Detection and Prevention of Identity-Based Bullying

Although there are some books that begin to talk about issues related to bullying, there are few texts that directly take on bullying as a social justice issue. This book is on the cutting edge of the field and will help guide much of the content for anti-bullying programming in schools, and create school and social policy that is lacking in this area.
—*Toni Zimmerman, Colorado State University, USA*

Bullying in schools has become the focus of a growing body of literature; however, much of that work diminishes the role of social context, social identities, and social prejudices despite extensive research evidence suggesting that many victims of bullying are targeted because of an aspect of their social identity. This book demonstrates how the prevention and intervention of this phenomenon, termed identity-based bullying, is a social justice issue.

Expanding beyond bullying prevention that focuses on individual perpetrators, the book examines identity-based bullying in schools as a microcosm of larger systemic tensions and conflicts. The author utilizes a social constructivist perspective to understand the experiences of children as active agents in their own lives. She also provides an international framework to describe the impact of culture, social structures, and politics from the U.S. and the U.K. Challenges and barriers to addressing identity-based bullying are explored and recommendations are made for best practices for teachers, administrators, and mental health professionals to prevent and respond to identity-based bullying.

Britney G Brinkman is Assistant Professor of Counseling Psychology at Chatham University, USA.

Researching Social Psychology

1 **Addressing Loneliness**
   Coping, Prevention and Clinical Interventions
   Edited by Ami Sha'ked & Ami Rokach

2 **Qualitative Research Methods in Consumer Psychology**
   Ethnography and Culture
   Edited by Paul M.W. Hackett

3 **Detection and Prevention of Identity-Based Bullying**
   Social Justice Perspectives
   Britney G Brinkman

Detection and Prevention of Identity-Based Bullying
Social Justice Perspectives

Britney G Brinkman

LONDON AND NEW YORK

First published 2016 by Routledge

2 Park Square, Milton Park, Abingdon, Oxon OX14 4RN
711 Third Avenue, New York, NY 10017, USA

Routledge is an imprint of the Taylor & Francis Group, an informa business

First issued in paperback 2017

Copyright © 2016 Taylor & Francis

The right of Britney G Brinkman to be identified as author of this work has been asserted by her in accordance with sections 77 and 78 of the Copyright, Designs and Patents Act 1988.

All rights reserved. No part of this book may be reprinted or reproduced or utilised in any form or by any electronic, mechanical, or other means, now known or hereafter invented, including photocopying and recording, or in any information storage or retrieval system, without permission in writing from the publishers.

Notice:
Product or corporate names may be trademarks or registered trademarks, and are used only for identification and explanation without intent to infringe.

Library of Congress Cataloging-in-Publication Data
Brinkman, Britney G, author.
  Detection and prevention of identity-based bullying : social justice perspectives / by Britney G Brinkman.
    pages cm. — (Researching social psychology ; 3)
  Includes bibliographical references and index.
  1. Bullying—Social aspects. 2. Bullying—Prevention. 3. Group identity. 4. Discrimination. I. Title.
  BF637.B85B75 2015
  302.34'3—dc23
  2015019763

ISBN: 978-0-415-71952-0 (hbk)
ISBN: 978-1-138-08592-3 (pbk)

Typeset in Sabon
by Apex CoVantage, LLC

*To Maddie, Ellie, Esther, Sabina, Jamie, Pursy, and Knox,
may you always let your inner light shine.
And
for every child whose life has been touched
by identity-based bullying.*

Contents

	Acknowledgments	ix
1	Defining Identity-Based Bullying	1
2	Examining Identity-Based Bullying as a Social Justice Issue	22
3	Understanding Identity-Based Bullying Through a Social Constructivist Framework	39
4	Cultural Factors Influencing Identity-Based Bullying	55
5	Educational Structures and Policies Impacting Identity-Based Bullying	70
6	Challenges and Barriers to Addressing Identity-Based Bullying	84
7	Recommendations for Best Practices to Prevent and Respond to Identity-Based Bullying	102
8	Conclusion	122
	Appendix: Useful Websites	131
	Index	135

Acknowledgments

This book would not have been possible without the assistance and support of many wonderful people.

First, I must thank Stacy Noto at Routledge Press, who initially approached me about my work and suggested that I submit the proposal for this book. Without your vision, this project would never have happened. Thank you also to Christina Chronister and the other staff at Routledge Press for helping this book come to fruition.

I am very appreciative to my department and home institution, which provided encouragement and support throughout the project.

This book was supported by the American Association of University Women through their American Summer/Short-Term Research Publication Grant. I am incredibly grateful for the generosity of the AAUW. The funding they provided allowed me to dedicate my time to the project in the way it deserved.

So many people assisted with the process of gathering information for the book. Thank you to all members of my Psychology of Gender Research Team whose hard work throughout the years has allowed many projects to flourish. I am especially thankful to the research assistants who helped with this project, including Sarah Goldberg, Jason Lucarelli, Erin Simpson, Caroline Zieth, Shawna Buerk, Evalyn Grey, and Kayla Kuykendall. Special thanks to Monica Thornhill who assisted in numerous ways on the project and whose attention to detail was invaluable. Kelly Rabenstein Donohoe was instrumental in the implementation of the FAIR+ program and worked with me on the early process of bridging my work in social justice with anti-bullying programs in schools. Your warmth, intelligence, and humor have always inspired me and made me proud.

I am so thankful to Lauren Manning, Keely Hirsch, Aliya Khan, and Alicia Haley for meticulously reading chapters of the book and providing me with excellent feedback. Thank you for braving even the very rough drafts. I am grateful also to my good friend Gail Wolfe who supported me and encouraged me throughout the book writing process. Our conversations about social justice in schools were invaluable in furthering my thinking for this book.

Acknowledgments

A warm thank you to B.B.B. and F.B.B. for the steadfast support.

To Anthony Isacco, who is my #1 cheerleader. Our collaboration on the Psychology of Gender Research Team is one of the best parts of my job. Thank you for being a colleague and friend.

To Lee Rosén, without whose mentorship I would not be where I am today. The opportunities I had to observe you work with children were some of the most inspirational moments of my educational experience. Thank you for always believing in me.

Thank you to my dear friend Deanna Hamilton, who has read much of the book and provided insightful and meaningful feedback. Your faith in me kept me moving when my own was lagging. I never imagined that I would be so lucky to have such a good friend and colleague in one person.

Thank you to Lindsay Butterfield for a friendship so true it cannot be dampened by distance or time—it reminds me of what really matters in life.

I want to express my deepest gratitude to my wonderful community of friends and neighbors who endured many "book-themed" dinners and celebrations while I was working on this project. This was a ploy to trick myself that writing a book would be more fun than terrifying. Thank you all for making this a reality. I am particularly grateful to Alicia Haley, Allison Haley, and Harmony Sullivan who offer me ongoing support and encouragement. Thank you for accepting me just as I am and for welcoming me into your families. Each of you is an inspirational model of what it means to be a strong, authentic, and loving woman. Your daughters are lucky to have you.

For my father, whose love, support, and sacrifices allowed me to achieve my dreams. If all children had fathers like you, the world would be a more loving and peaceful space. Thank you for always believing in me and teaching me even at a young age that girls can be anything they want to be. To my mother, my first role model, who taught me what it meant to be a feminist and how to turn righteous rage into social change. Thank you for your courage in following your dreams and paving the way for me. Thank you to my brothers for their support, intellectually stimulating conversations, and endless humor.

I am so grateful to my loving husband, Sam Burns, for his ongoing faith in me and unwavering support of my work. In addition to reading the entire book and offering me valuable feedback, he did everything he could to provide me with the time I needed to finish the project and reminded me that self-care is a thing, even when writing a book. His passion, humor, and steadfastness make my life better every day.

Finally, I want to thank all educators, mental health professionals, administrators, and scholars who are working to eradicate identity-based bullying and to make schools a safer space for all children.

1 Defining Identity-Based Bullying

In September of 2011, openly gay, 14-year-old Jamey Rodmeyer committed suicide after experiencing nearly constant homophobic bullying (O'Connor, 2011). In April 2012, 14-year-old Kenneth Weishuhn committed suicide after being bullied for being gay—having experienced in-person teasing, being the target of a Facebook hate group, and even receiving death threats (Johnson, 2012). These are just two of many similar tragic stories of youth committing suicide after being bullying. Of course, the factors impacting youth suicide are complex, but research has shown that identity-based bullying can play a role. Gay male youth who are repeatedly bullied are especially likely to contemplate or attempt suicide (Friedman, Koeske, Silvestre, Korr, & Sites, 2006).

In the United States, bullying has been a topic of growing concern among school administrators, scholars, parents, and advocacy groups since 1999, when two students attacked Columbine High School and killed 12 classmates and one teacher (and injured many others) before taking their own lives (Lamb, 2008). The aftermath of the tragedies at Columbine included desperate attempts to understand why it happened, with the hopes of preventing future cases. Some people focused on violence in the media, others on gun control—but many learned of the incessant bullying that the two attackers had experienced and began to wonder what role that played in their decision to commit such a violent act. The literature regarding bullying has grown since 1999, and many school districts across the United States added anti-bullying programs in response to concerns regarding school violence.

WHY WE SHOULD BE CONCERNED ABOUT BULLYING

Over a decade after the tragedy in Colorado, bullying prevention gained fresh attention in the United States in March 2011 when President Obama hosted the first ever White House anti-bullying conference. At this conference, Obama emphasized the need for schools to take bullying seriously, saying "If there is one goal of this conference, it is to dispel the myth that bullying is just a harmless rite of passage or an inevitable part of growing up"

(Shepherd, 2011). Bullying is a problem in most schools and in most countries, including the U.K. and the U.S. Within Great Britain, 75% of 2,722 students surveyed reported experiencing bullying but less than 50% said that their schools had an anti-bullying policy (Katz, Buchanan, & Bream, 2001).

Children who are targets of bullying experience a number of negative consequences, including depression, suicidal behavior, low self-esteem, negative health outcomes, truancy, and negative impacts on academic performance (See Chapter 2 of this volume for more information). Some research has found that children who experience bullying have poorer social and emotional adjustment, report feelings of loneliness, greater difficulty making friends, and poor relationships with classmates (Nansel et al., 2001). The pervasiveness of bullying and its impact on targets make it necessary for mental health professionals, school officials, and parents to be concerned.

Attending to Social Identities

Although many anti-bullying programs have been found to be effective at preventing some types of bullying, most have neglected to address the impact of social identity on bullying—choosing instead to focus on bullying in a decontextualized manner. Some scholars and advocates have argued that this approach to bullying is insufficient. Much of the bullying that takes place in-person and online is based on an individual's social identity (Wessler & De Andrade, 2006), and subgroups that have especially high frequencies of victimization include students with disabilities or those who identify as lesbian, gay, bisexual, or transgender (Swearer, Espelage, Vaillancourt, & Hymel, 2010). As a result, scholars and educational advocates have called for anti-bullying programs to pay greater attention to gender, race, sexual orientation, and ethnicity (Jenson, Dieterich, Brisson, Bender, & Powell, 2010). In fact, shortly after the tragedy at Columbine High School, scholars argued that a complete understanding of the incident required recognizing the impact of masculinity. Katz and Jhally (1999) asserted that the bullying experienced by the shooters occurred within a context in which strength and dominance were celebrated masculine ideals and those who did not measure up were subjected to criticism and bullying. Scholars who have examined this case and similar school shootings have argued that many school shooters experienced relentless bullying based on perceptions that they did not meet others' expectations of masculinity and thus attempted to "prove" their masculinity through violence (Kimmel & Mahler, 2003; Klein, 2012).

So, why am *I* writing *this* book? While I am concerned about bullying and the impact it has on children and adolescents, it was not my main focus as a clinician or researcher. In fact, I entered the world of anti-bullying research in an unexpected way—I came to this work through my focus on social justice issues and children's experiences of discrimination. My doctoral dissertation consisted of implementing and evaluating a program (Fairness for All Individuals through Respect) in schools that taught children about social identities (Brinkman, Jedinak, Rosén, & Zimmerman, 2011). The program examines gender, ethnicity, and social class and explores how students learn about these (and other) aspects of identity. Much of the program explores how kids treat each other if they do not conform to stereotypes or how they might treat people who are different from them and encourages children to treat everyone with respect (Zimmerman, Aberle, & Krafchick, 2006).

After graduate school, I continued to work on this program (and others like it) and contacted schools to collaborate with them on social justice programming. It was during this time that I became increasingly aware that some educational professionals were linking social justice programming with anti-bullying work—at least conceptually. I was told by some schools that they had no need for the programming I was doing because they already utilized an anti-bullying program. Others asked about ways to integrate the program into their existing anti-bullying framework. At first, I was somewhat hesitant to do this, as I thought that discrimination and harassment are so qualitatively different from bullying that they should be addressed separately. I was not alone in this thinking, and many notable scholars have expressed concerns about conflating bullying and harassment (Brown, Chesney-Lind, & Stein, 2007; Meyer, 2009; Ringrose & Renold; 2010). I was worried, as were many of these scholars, that the bullying framework may be used to ignore or dismiss deeper conversations about sexism, racism, classism, and homophobia in schools.

However, as I continued working to implement social justice programming in schools, it became clear to me that there was a need to address identity-based bullying in schools. To do so, it was necessary to find a way to bridge the worlds of anti-bullying research and antidiscrimination research. It is my hope that this book will begin conversations about identity issues where they are absent, further discussions in schools where they already occur, and provide resources for scholars, educators, and administrators who are working to eradicate identity-based bullying.

WHAT IS IDENTITY-BASED BULLYING?

This book focuses on detecting and preventing a particular subset of behaviors termed identity-based bullying. *Identity-based bullying* is used to describe any form of bullying related to the characteristics considered unique to a child's actual or perceived social identity. This type of bullying occurs when an individual is targeted because of an aspect of his or her social identity (e.g., a gay child being shoved in the hallway) and/or when the content of the bullying focuses on identity variables, even if it does not accurately reflect that child's identity (e.g., a child being called a racist name). In their report for the Equality and Human Rights commission, Tippett, Houlston, and Smith (2010) assert that identity-based bullying is unique, because it reflects negative attitudes about an entire group, not only the individual

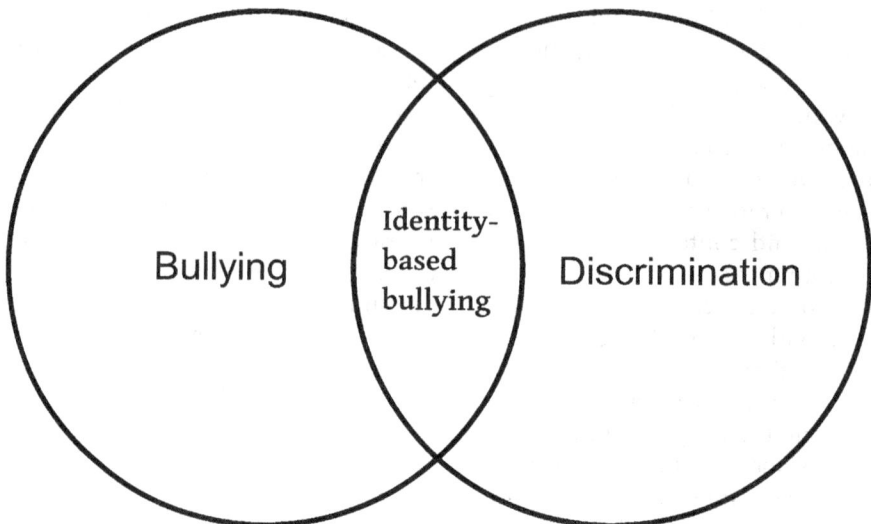

Figure 1.1 The Relation of Bullying, Discrimination, and Identity-Based Bullying

being targeted. The term *prejudice-based bullying* is also sometimes used to describe these behaviors. In this book, I will most often use the term identity-based bullying or refer to specific subtypes, such as gender-based bullying or homophobic bullying.

Bullying Versus Harassment

The current academic literature (be it within psychology, law, education, or social work) about bullying is growing, but several complications have arisen regarding terminology. What constitutes bullying, and how does it differ from harassment based on discrimination? *Discrimination* is an action that treats people unfairly because of their membership in a particular social group. Identity-based bullying includes bullying behaviors that are rooted in discrimination; therefore, in this book, I integrate the research on bullying with the research on discrimination to develop a better understanding of the events occurring in children's lives. While this book will not extensively address bullying that is not identity-based or behaviors rooted in discrimination that are not bullying, understanding the factors that contribute to these two phenomenon is essential for preventing identity-based bullying.

The most common definitions of bullying define it as a subset of aggression. It is characterized by an imbalance of power between target and perpetrator and includes repeated incidents that can lead to feelings of fear and intimidation on the part of the target (Olweus, 1993; Orpinas & Horne, 2006; Rigby, 2004). Differences in power can be seen through physical strength, social capital, or social skills. While this definition may be useful for researchers, there is often more ambiguity involved for clinicians and educators who work in schools and try to identify bullying in day-to-day life. For example, it may be difficult for adults to know when children are engaging in rough play versus bullying. *Rough play* can include playful teasing or arguing within the context of imaginary play (Orpinas & Horne, 2006). However, this play crosses the line into bullying if it becomes hurtful and is continued. Some researchers argue that, in addition to the abuse of power and intensity and duration of behaviors, actions should only be labeled as bullying when there is intent to harm another person (Fried & Soslan, 2011). Unfortunately it is quite challenging to assess another's intentions (e.g., to be playful versus hurtful), and children may underestimate the impact of their behaviors, thus causing harm to their peers even if they do not intend to do so.

These general definitions of bullying do not clearly differentiate between behaviors that are labeled bullying and those that should be termed harassment. Meyer (2009) defines *harassment* as "biased behaviors, intentional or unintentional, targeted at an individual or no specific targets" (p. 3). These differences matter, as bullying and harassment can have different antecedents and consequences. Distinguishing between bullying and harassment is also important because schools may have different legal responsibilities in how they attend to these behaviors. For example, in the United States, children have a legal right to protection against discrimination based on their sex, and schools are required to take particular actions to address such discrimination if it occurs (see Chapter 5 for an exploration of the laws in the U.S and U.K. that relate to identity-based bullying).

Despite the differences, Meyer (2009) asserts that there is overlap in discriminatory harassment and bullying and some incidents would be classified as both. Unfortunately, this overlap is not always recognized, and instead some schools focus only on bullying. After interviewing primary and secondary school children in the United Kingdom, Ringrose and Renold (2010) argue that most discourses about bullying minimize the power relations within schools related to gender, ethnicity, social class, and sexuality. The term *bullying* may be used in place of terms such as sexism, racism, and homophobia as a way to avoid discussing systemic problems rooted in cultural stereotypes and oppression (Brown et al., 2007; Strauss, 2012). Bullying frameworks that have taken an identity-neutral approach often focus on bullying as a problem between an individual bully and a victim and minimize or ignore prejudice-based interactions among children. As a result, students and schools may be attending less to racism, sexism, homophobia, classism, sexual harassment, and similar concerns while turning their attention to bullying.

A body of work is beginning to emerge that examines the connections between bullying and harassment. For example, Espelage and Swearer (2008) explore the intersections of homophobia and bullying, and Dewitt (2012) examines harassment and bullying of LGBT students in schools. Meyer (2009) explores sexism and homophobia in schools, examining how bullying and harassment interconnect and diverge. Richardson and Miles (2008) examine racism and bullying within schools, and McNamara (2013) analyzes bullying of students with disabilities. I build upon the work that these (and other scholars) have done to distinguish between bullying and harassment, while also bridging these two areas of research to analyze cases of identity-based bullying, which exist in the intersection of the two.

TYPES OF IDENTITY-BASED BULLYING

In the following text, I detail some of the specific types of identity-based bullying and provide research about how each type of bullying may present itself. While the following sections focus on one aspect of identity, it is essential to keep in mind that each child is a combination of their different identities. For example, Price (1999) explores the importance of the intersections of race and gender in his examinations of the experiences of young black men in school. The impact of intersecting identities goes beyond being cumulative (e.g., a Latina adolescent from a working class family might experience three types of identity-based bullying) and may result in qualitatively different experiences for individuals. In a number of British schools, Duncan (1999) noticed the intersections of ethnicity and gender in the experiences of the boys. The African Caribbean boys were assumed to be macho, exciting, and antiauthoritarian, while the Asian boys were seen as less masculine, shy, and complicit with authority. The boys who were assumed to be more masculine experienced less gender-based bullying. Although children are a compilation of their identities, they may see one aspect of their identity as more salient than another, particularly if one aspect of identity places them in the majority group, while another makes them a member of an oppressed group (e.g., white girls) (Turner & Brown, 2007).

Gender Identity

Children reinforce gender normative behavior among each other using exclusion, teasing, and physical and emotional harassment (Lamb, Bigler, Liben, & Green, 2009). Brown, Alabi, Huynh, and Masten (2011) found that 76% of the children in their study were aware of at least one instance of gender bias. One of the most common forms of gender-based bullying against girls is sexual harassment, including repeated unwanted sexual comments, jokes, and gestures, as well as physical harassment (being touched or grabbed). Most accounts suggest that sexual harassment is rampant within the United States and the United Kingdom (and many other countries as well, see the 2008 international study by Amnesty International that examined the frequency of sexual harassment of girls in schools around the world). While most of the research about sexual harassment of youth has focused on adolescents, there are documented cases of sexual harassment in elementary schools and even preschools (Strauss, 2012). A 2011 study by the American Association of University Women found that 48% of students (56% of girls and 40% of boys) reported being sexually harassed at school. While both boys and girls reported experiencing sexual harassment, girls indicated more experiences of physical harassment than did boys. A vast majority of these students (87%) indicated being negatively affected by the harassment. This is a particularly important figure, because many teachers dismiss the behavior as "normal" adolescent male behavior (Eder, Evans, & Stephen, 1995), and schools rarely take sexual harassment seriously (Strauss, 2012).

Schools may also reflect attitudes about a sexual double standard, whereby boys are rewarded for their (perceived) sexual prowess, and girls are punished for their (perceived) sexual experience. One form of identity-based bullying capitalizes on this assumption in the form of name-calling of girls and attempts to damage their sexual reputation. Some of the gender-based bullying that occurs in schools takes the form of *slut shaming* or *slut bashing* (Lamb, 2001; Tolman, 2002). According to Klein (2012), slut bashing includes incidents where one "questions the sexual legitimacy of a target and then lashes out at her with vicious names conveying she is worthless" (p. 8). Slut shaming can involve bullying where a girl is targeted with insults based on her actual or perceived sexual activity. It reinforces expectations that girls should not engage in sexual activity and encourages a double standard in which boys can be sexually active (Tanenbaum, 2000). Of particular horror is slut shaming of girls who have experienced sexual assault by teachers or peer(s). Girls who come forward about these experiences may find themselves bombarded with online and in-person bullying in the form of comments calling them sluts and blaming them for their mistreatment, because of the shape of their bodies, the way they dress, or their sexual reputations.

Girls also are targeted with bullying that includes other forms of sexism, such as hearing derogatory comments and experiencing ostracism. These forms of gender-based bullying are directly linked to traditional gender stereotypes, which emphasize unequal power relationships between girls and boys (and women and men). Within the U.S. legal framework, some of these experiences may be classified as sexual harassment, because they include harassment or bullying based on gender, a form of sexual harassment that is sometimes referred to as sexist harassment (Strauss, 2012). In one study of British schools, girls of all ages reported concerns about the way they were treated by the boys, being called names and being sexualized by the boys. Many of the younger boys thought it was acceptable to call girls derogatory names (like cow or bitch) if a girl challenged a boy's perceived authority (Duncan, 1999). Boys may bully girls in order to assert power and conform to a framework of masculinity that emphasizes dominance (Klein, 2012).

While these behaviors may occur at any age, middle school is a time when many adolescents are developing their ideas about gender, sexuality, and power, and boys may aggressively attempt to assert power over girls (Eder, Evans, & Stephen, 1995). Schools rarely challenge these unequal power dynamics, but more often reproduce them by modeling these power imbalances in their social structures and the interactions among teachers and administrators and between teachers and students (for more discussion of this, see Chapters 2 and 3 in this book).

Girls may also engage in identity-based bullying against other girls. Some of this bullying takes the form of relational aggression, which includes behaviors intended to harm someone by hurting their relationships with others or damaging their sense of inclusion. Relational aggression can include sabotage, gossiping, and trying to ruin someone's reputation. Some scholars have suggested that girls use this form of aggression more than boys do (Crick & Grotpeter, 1995; Wiseman, 2002). Brown (2005) argues that relational aggression is more common among girls because "it's a strategy used more often by those with less power because it protects one from retaliation or from punishment by those in control. It's a very useful strategy for girls because it provides a cover for unfeminine emotions like anger" (p. 16). Not all incidents of relational aggression or indirect bullying would classify as identity-based bullying, but some relational aggression is related to gender-role identity (Crothers, Field, & Kolbert, 2005). Relational aggression may be used as a form of punishment against girls who are perceived to violate stereotypical feminine-role expectations.

Boys' experiences of gender-based bullying can be similar to girls; and the most basic definition is the same. It includes bullying in which a boy is targeted because of his gender (or the way in which he presents his gender) and/or the content of the bullying denigrates a boy's masculinity. While boys can and do experience sexual harassment, scholarship suggests that boys are more likely to experience gender-based bullying that implies a boy is not "adequately" meeting others' definitions of masculinity. As many gender theorists have discussed (e.g. Kimmel, 2009; Klein, 2006; Pollack, 1998; and others), expectations to conform to hegemonic masculinity, the rejection of femininity, and homophobia are all intertwined. Schools often encourage violent and traditional interpretations of masculinity (Harber, 2009), and boys may acquire social capital in schools by engaging in behaviors that mirror and reinforce these definitions. Many schools have male peer hierarchies in which individual boys try to move up the hierarchy (and try to avoid moving down the hierarchy) by engaging in traditional masculinity behaviors, such as athletics, fighting, distancing themselves from homosexuality, and being dominant in relationships with girls (Klein, 2006). Identity-based bullying is one way these hierarchies are maintained.

Some scholars have argued that boys (and later men) police each other's performances of masculinity through bullying (Kimmel, 2009; Pollack, 1998). Studies of boys in the U.S. and the U.K. have shown that boys are targeted with gender-based bullying if they appear to be too feminine or do not conform to stereotypes about masculinity (Duncan, 1999; Heinze & Horn, 2014). Boys who lack ability in sports, who obey the teachers, or who do well in school may all be targets of identity-based bullying. In addition, accusations of femininity can be used as a form of teasing or bullying, even of boys who do conform to gender stereotypes. One common example of this is the use of the phrase "throwing like a girl" as a way to insult boys (Anthamatten, 2014). These jaunts not only offend boys who are the target of them (and send the message that they are not being masculine *enough*) but also send a message to girls about their relative position and value in society.

Much of the gender-based bullying against boys comes in the form of homophobic teasing, taunts, and jeers. While some boys are targeted because of their actual sexual orientation (which I discuss in more detail below), some of this bullying happens because a boy is not stereotypically masculine—regardless of his real or perceived sexual orientation. Some boys are bullied because they are assumed to be heterosexual but "failing" at it. In the United Kingdom, this pattern was observed in a school where the younger boys were teased because of their lack of sexual development and experience (Duncan, 1999). Pascoe (2007) describes observing a high school boy in the U.S. who was teased and bullied by his peers and the teachers because he did not meet the standards of masculinity set at that school. He was targeted because of his style of dress, the way he walked, and the way he talked. Most of the teasing related to his assumed inability to display sexual prowess toward girls.

Students who identify as gender nonconforming or transgender are especially at risk of experiencing identity-based bullying (Strauss, 2012). Transgender students include those who feel that their biological sex does not match their self-identified gender. Some girls and boys who do not fit into traditional stereotypes of masculinity or femininity are referred to as gender nonconforming or gender variant. They identify as male or female but do not restrict themselves to traditionally masculine or feminine attire or activities. A 2009 study indicated that 65% of transgender students felt unsafe in schools because of how they expressed their gender (Greytak, Kosciw, & Diaz, 2009). A similar U.S. based report of the climate of schools found that 64% of LGBT students experienced verbal harassment because of their gender expression (Kosciw, Greytak, Bartkiewicz, Boesen, & Palmer, 2012). While many research studies and reports have examined the experiences of transgender youth in conjunction with lesbian, gay, and bisexual (LGB) youth, many transgender students face bullying specific to their transgender identity (McGuire, Anderson, Toomey, & Russell, 2010). Some research suggests that boys who do not conform to stereotypes about gender may experience more social repercussions than girls who do not conform (although some might argue that they experience different types of repercussions). In one study, Heinze and Horn (2014) found that gender nonconforming boys experienced social exclusion but gender nonconforming girls did not. Girls who behave in gender atypical ways are sometimes labeled (and label themselves) as tomboys. This term is rarely used as a pejorative and might even give a girl social status in a school (Pascoe, 2007).

Sexual Orientation

One of the most common reasons that children are targeted for bullying is their actual or perceived sexual orientation. Children and adolescents who are out as lesbian, gay, or bisexual (LGB), as well as kids who are assumed to be LGB, are often the targets of teasing, ostracism, and even physical violence. Studies of identity-based bullying of students who identify as gay, lesbian, or bisexual have found that anywhere from 25% to 84% report experiencing bullying, ranging from verbal harassment (the most common) to physical harassment (Elze, 2003; Kosciw, et.al, 2012; Poteat & Espelage, 2005). Some of the bullying can be very extreme. In fact, 17% of 1,145 gay teens in Britain reported experiencing death threats from classmates (Bawden, 2008), and some gay students experience physical violence (Kosciw et al., 2012; Pascoe, 2007). It is important to note that these numbers are likely lower than the actual frequencies, as many youth do not report their experiences to adults. One British survey of 13–15-year-olds and their teachers found that two-thirds of students and three-fourths of teachers witnessed some form of homophobic bullying, but only 13% of students were familiar with any school policies designed to address it (Richardson, 2004). One result of the lack of school policies may be that students neglect to report experiences of homophobic bullying for fear of retaliation or lack of faith that anything will be done to effectively address the behavior.

Some have argued that gay male youth experience more identity-based bullying than lesbians (Strauss, 2012). In some schools, girls who identify as lesbians find greater social acceptance than boys who identify as gay. In my own research with adolescent girls, some reported their perception that their high school was more accepting of lesbian relationships than of gay male relationships. However, this does not mean that lesbians are never subjected to identity-based bullying. One qualitative study of lesbian young women revealed they frequency experienced bullying in the form of isolation, harassment, and pressures to conform to social norms (Pendragon, 2010). In one school, girls in the Gay-Straight Alliance reported that they were consistently harassed by their classmates, their posters for events were torn down, and their announcements were ignored (Pascoe, 2007).

In addition to LGB students being targeted with various forms of bullying because of their actual or perceived sexual orientation, bullying that uses accusations that one is gay or lesbian as an insult is a form of identity-based bullying. In one study, boys and girls told Pascoe (2007) that being called *fag* was the worst insult a boy could receive. She found that the term *gay* was also often used as a slur but usually with different context. Among the students she studied, the term *gay* was used to refer to anything a student perceived to be uncool or stupid. It was applied to people and objects, while the term fag was used as a more limited and targeted form of bullying.

Ethnicity, Nationality, and Religion

Identity-based bullying also occurs on the basis of a child's ethnicity, nationality, or religion. Within the United Kingdom, students who are Asian, Hindu, Indian Muslim, and Pakistani have all reported racial-based bullying (Boulton & Smith, 1992; Eslea & Mukhtar, 2000). By early adolescence, a majority of ethnic minority children in the United States have experienced discrimination from their peers (Brown et al., 2011). Much of this discrimination is in the form of identity-based bullying and includes verbal insults and racial slurs (Simons et al., 2002). Over 52% of African American adolescents in one study reported being insulted, called a name, or harassed because of their racial identity (Sellers, Copeland-Linder, Martin, & Lewis, 2006). In my own research at a school with predominantly African American children, many reported experiencing racial-based bullying in the form of being called the "N-word," being excluded, and being teased. One student (fifth grade, female) talked about her experiences at a previous school.

> I have been treated badly because of the color of my skin. Because I went to a Catholic school, and me and my brother and sister were there. And then there weren't many kids with colored skin and they used to tease me. They used to play games and they said I wasn't allowed to play (see Brinkman & Manning, in press, for more information about this study).

Much of the research conducted in the United States about ethnic discrimination against students has focused on students who identify as African American/Black or Latino, with less research about the experiences of Asian Americans. Zhou and Xiong (2005) argue that children of Asian immigrants have often been neglected by researchers because it is assumed that they will be successful. This assumption may be related to the relatively high levels of socio-economic status (SES) experienced by Asian Americans compared to African Americans and/or Latinos. Alternatively, it may result from researchers' internalization of the *model minority* stereotype, a stereotype in which Asian Americans are assumed to be affluent and educated and possessing a strong work ethic (Taylor & Stern, 1997). The relative lack of research about Asian children's experiences of racial-based bullying should not be interpreted to mean that they do not occur. More research is needed in this area.

While it is important to note that religion is distinct from ethnicity and nationality, children (and adults) often conflate the two in terms of treating another person in a discriminatory way. For example, following the attack on the World Trade Center in New York City in 2001, children living in the

United States who were from the Middle East (or whose parents or grandparents were from the Middle East) experienced bullying based on others' perceptions that they were Muslim (Holcomb, 2011). This conflation of ethnicity and religion has been slow to dissipate in the United States (see Chapter 4 for more information). One study of British students found that some bullying of Hindu, Indian Muslim, and Pakistani children was related to the places where they worshipped, suggesting that these children may have been targeted for their religious and ethnic identities (Eslea & Mukhtar, 2000). Further, there is a long history of tension in Northern Ireland between Catholics and Protestants, and children within these communities may be bullied as a result of their family's religious ties. Children in segregated schools in Northern Ireland are less likely to have cross-group contact and friendships than children in integrated schools (Stringer et al., 2009).

Social Class

Social class is an aspect of social identity that is less often discussed than other types of identity (gender, ethnicity, sexual orientation) in regard to experiences of identity-based bullying in schools. This is partially a result of the fact that schools are often mostly homogenous with respect to social class (see Chapter 5 for more information about the ways in which school systems are often divided by social class). Despite this relative homogeneity, cliques in schools often form around social class. Students utilize status markers, such as the brands of clothing kids wear, the types of cars they or their parents drive, or even where they go on vacation to determine which groups children belong to. Children who do not have the "right" status symbol for that environment (often shifting brands and items) may be teased, harassed, or excluded from activities (Klein, 2006). In societies that emphasize consumerism as a way of gaining power and prestige, children may seek out cultural capital by emphasizing social class privilege (Klein, 2012).

Some class-based bullying occurs in direct interactions among peers, in which children are targeted or bullied because of their social class. Liu, Soleck, Hopps, Dunston, and Pickett (2004) argue that there are three types of interpersonal classism. All three of these may present themselves in schools as a type of identity-based bullying. The first type includes upward classism, in which individuals from higher SES groups are teased or stereotyped. The second type is downward classism, which includes discrimination against individuals from working-class or poor families. Lower SES kids might be called names or experience exclusion and ostracism. Students from upper-class families might avoid interactions with kids from lower SES families. Finally, lateral classism occurs when people from a similar social class point out that others should behave in a way that it more congruent with the expectations of that class. Students might tease others who are from the same social class if they behave in ways they do not feel is congruent with the expectations of their class.

Social class bullying may also take the form of derogatory comments about particular neighborhoods or people who live in those neighborhoods. Many regions have local vernacular or nicknames for people from a particular neighborhood or section of a city. Phrases such as being on the "wrong side of the tracks" suggest attitudes that there are geographically superior (and inferior) places to live. Social class bullying might take the form of calling someone a slur that refers to a poorer area of town or simply making fun of an area of town.

Social class can be an invisible identity or one that is not readily obvious to others. Children may learn ways to pass so that people assume their social class matches the majority of those around them (poorer children may attempt to appear middle class, wealthy children might downplay their resources or not talk about their parents' occupations). Because of this, class-based bullying may have effects on individuals without the perpetrator's awareness. Kids who are teasing one student because of his or her class may not know that another peer shares the same identity.

Ability/Disability

Students with disabilities may be at particular risk of being bullied by their peers and may receive less support from teachers when bullying occurs. One study suggests up to 80% of children on the autism spectrum have been bullied (Ability Path, 2011). In a United Kingdom study of students with disabilities, 83% of the students reported being bullied about their disability (Norwich & Kelly, 2004). The bullying included being called names (such as *dumb* or *thick*), being teased when they struggled to read or write, and even experiencing physical violence. Students with certain disabilities (such as ADHD and Asperger's syndrome) may act in an impulsive manner or lack social skills. As a result, these students may be perceived as annoying (by both students and teachers), be bullied by other kids, and receive less empathy from teachers. Some scholars refer to these children as "provocative" victims (McNamara, 2013). When these students try to get help or report being bullied, they are often told to change the way they behave. "If you just kept quiet, they wouldn't tease you," teachers might say. Children with disabilities often get in trouble when they respond to or retaliate against bullying. Because of their lack of social skills, these children may be less able to temper their reactions and may behave disruptively when they are being bullied, which can result in disciplinary action against them for their behavior.

Children with disabilities may be targeted because of their perceived vulnerability and their differences from typical students. One study found that preschool-age children preferred photos of children without physical disabilities over those shown with some type of adaptive equipment (like wheelchairs) (Huckstadt & Shutts, 2014). Students with disabilities may be ostracized from their peers, excluded from social activities, and become the target of jokes or pranks. Much of the teasing that is directed at students with disabilities takes the form of mimicking a student's impairment (e.g., pretending to use sign language, or mimicking a speech impediment) (McNamara, 2013). Students may become targets of bullying if they are placed in more restrictive classrooms or self-contained environments than if they are in inclusive and collaborative classrooms (McNamara, 2013). Norwich and Kelly (2004) looked at students who attended mainstream schools and special needs schools. They found that children who attended special needs schools experienced more bullying outside of schools by their peers than students who attended mainstream schools. While additional research is needed to fully understand this finding, it is possible that students who spend some of their time in classroom experiences with typical students develop allies and friends who support them.

PERPETRATORS OF IDENTITY-BASED BULLYING

Most scholarship on bullying focuses on nonfamilial peers as the potential perpetrators. In this book, I will focus on incidents of bullying perpetrated by peers, but I will also discuss the ways in which adults may contribute to or confront identity-based bullying. Lots of research has attempted to understand why some children may be more likely than others to engage in bullying, often focusing on individual characteristics, such as personality, family experiences (especially abusive ones), past experience as a victim of bullying, and others (Espelage & Swearer, 2004; Fried & Soslan, 2011; Ma, 2001). While this is certainly important information (for example, this helps to identify children who are at most risk of becoming bullies and to implement programming for them), it does not necessarily examine the conditions under which identity-based bullying occurs. In this book, I focus on examining the larger context in which identity-based bullying exists: Why does anyone engage in this behavior, and what can be done to prevent it? I encourage those interested in learning more about the individual characteristics associated with perpetrating bullying behavior to read the work of Orpinas and Horne (2006), Espelage and Swearer (2004), and others.

Although I will include specific examples of incidents of identity-based bullying to illuminate what the experiences are like for the individuals involved, I will also focus on groups of children who may be more likely to perpetrate or be targeted with various types of identity-based bullying. Perpetrators may be members of an out-group (e.g., middle-class children bullying working-class children) or in-group members (e.g., boys bullying other boys). Further, bullying perpetrated by different groups might serve slightly different functions. Boys who call other boys gay may be attempting to protect themselves from bullying by affirming their conformity to masculinity and by distancing themselves from homosexuality (see Chapter 3). In contrast, girls who call boys gay for not conforming to such stereotypical expectations may do so because of the ideas and values they have internalized about what it means to be "masculine." They may also be looking for a way to feel powerful in a social system that often denies them power because of their gender identity. Brown (2005) argues that girls' aggression, although often minimized or trivialized, should be examined within the context of patriarchy, exploring how girls attempt to protect their small piece of the "patriarchal pie" (p. 6).

I do not necessarily distinguish between *bullies* and *victims* as though any particular child occupies either role at all times. In fact, research on bullying in general suggests that many children who engage in bullying behavior were once victims themselves (Ma, 2001). Children may also be a target of identity-based bullying because of one aspect of their identity (e.g., ethnicity) and bully other children based on other aspects of identity (e.g., sexual orientation). Throughout the book I may use the terms *perpetrator, instigator*, or *bully* as well as *victim* or *target* depending upon the situation. I take as a starting place that any child may engage in bullying behavior or be bullied by others. I also explore the role of bystanders of bullying, those who are not directly engaged as either a target or perpetrator but are witnesses to the interaction. Bystanders may play various roles during such situations, ranging from endorsement of bullying to attempts to intervene, although many stay silent while witnessing these interactions, even when they do not agree with the behavior (Baldry, 2005; O'Connell, 1999). As I examine the system in which bullying occurs, I explore how bystanders are impacted by the behavior, as well as how they can impact the system through the choices they make during such incidents. (see Chapter 3 for more discussion of the roles children play).

OVERVIEW OF THE BOOK

Using the term "identity-based bullying" should not (and does not) preclude schools from attending to bullying that is not about identity or from addressing discrimination that does not take the form of bullying. It is about recognizing that there is often overlap between these two phenomena and encouraging social scientists to merge the literature of the two areas to better understand identity-based bullying. Practically, it allows teachers, clinicians, and administrators to develop policies and procedures that better recognize and effectively detect and prevent a class of behaviors that are frequent and harmful to those who experience and witness them.

Although there is a body of research exploring adults' experiences with bullying (e.g., Jenkins, Zapf, Winefield, & Sarris, 2012; Spurgeon, 1997), in this book I focus on the experiences of children and adolescents. At times I refer to my own direct research with children, occasionally including quotes from the children themselves (with names and identifying information changed to protect the children's identity). However, in some areas I refer to literature that has been conducted with adult samples in order to better explain a phenomenon. I also integrate research about adults when relevant in order to explore the structural issues surrounding identity-based bullying. In general, the book is intended to apply to a full age range of children and adolescents, but at times I will discuss findings that are especially relevant for a particular subgroup (e.g., preschoolers or high school students). I do not examine bullying explicitly from a stage model of development (e.g., Erikson, 1968), rather I utilize a social constructivist framework to understand the role identity-based bullying plays in children's identity development and acquisition of prejudicial attitudes.

Much of this book examines schools as a centralized location in which identity-based bullying occurs. This is not to say that bullying doesn't take place in other arenas, indeed LGB youth have reported that they experience bullying in a range of settings, including schools, homes, public places, the street and public transit, and cyberspace (Mishna, Newman, Daley, & Solomon, 2009). I focus on schools because: 1) most children spend a large proportion of their time within school systems; 2) many school systems are structured in such a way that they recreate and promote identity-based bullying; and 3) schools can be excellent epicenters for change, creating ripple effects throughout society. I encourage scholars, teachers, clinicians, and parents who are interested in identity-based bullying to apply this work in other areas as they see fit, as well as to adapt it as needed.

I predominantly focus on identity-based bullying that occurs through in-person interactions. However, it is important to note that many scholars and school systems are struggling with issues related to cyberbullying and the role that schools can and should play in intervening in this bullying format (Hinduja & Patchin, 2012). This book focuses on underlying causes of identity-based bullying, and as such, much of it can and does apply to cyberbullying, but most of the examples will be focused on in-person exchanges.

Within the book I discuss how identity-based bullying occurs within the United States and the United Kingdom. Scholars and educators within the U.K. are likely more familiar with the term *identity-based bullying* than those in the U.S. and have more policies defining it. By examining both nations, I am able to compare and contrast ways in which cultural, political, and social structures all influence identity-based bullying. The U.S. and U.K. provide interesting comparisons for each other, as they have many cultural similarities, while also maintaining important distinctions (e.g., in the structure of school systems). Throughout the book, I have sought to incorporate perspectives from both nations by integrating scholarship and news from each. However, it is important to acknowledge that as a researcher who lives and works within the United States, my perspective is situated within the U.S., and I am more familiar with the cultural experiences and scholarship from that country.

In Chapters 2 and 3, I describe the theoretical approaches that lay the foundation for my examination of identity-based bullying. First, I explain why effectively studying, identifying, tackling, and preventing identity-based bullying is a social justice imperative. I describe the traditions that have informed my understanding of social justice and present arguments for school systems to do more to promote a just world. In Chapter 3, I demonstrate that utilizing a social constructivist framework provides a deeper understanding of the impact of identity-based bullying on children's identity development. As this framework views children as active agents creating their own realities, it also provides a nuanced approach to developing prevention programming and encourages scholars to actively involve children in antidiscrimination work.

Within Chapters 4 and 5, I broaden the scope of discussion, examining the cultural, political, and structural factors that contribute to the etiology and persistence of identity-based bullying. In Chapter 4, I explore how cultural factors (including media, social policies, and public discourses) impact the development and reinforcement of identity-based bullying. Next (in Chapter 5), I explore educational laws, policies, and structure in both the U.S. and the U.K., focusing in particular on those issues that impact identity-based bullying.

In Chapters 6 and 7, I turn to the practical applications of theory. In Chapter 6, I describe the most common challenges psychologists, researchers, school administrators, and teachers might face when attempting to address identity-based bullying. Chapter 7 provides recommendations for best practices in addressing identity-based bullying. It describes what researchers, administrators, and school officials can do to better understand and prevent identity-based bullying, with case examples used to illustrate how to put the recommendations into place.

In the concluding chapter, I discuss future directions for identity-based bullying prevention and social justice work within and outside of schools. Last, there is a list of helpful organizations and websites.

Although the work can be challenging, deterring identity-based bullying and deconstructing the structural and social factors contributing to it is one course of action toward the creation of more just schools. I believe that educational institutions can do more than reinforce inequality—they can challenge the status quo and become diverse environments where children develop into active, engaged, global citizens. It is my hope that this book will serve as a resource for researchers, psychologists, and school officials who seek to create safer and more inclusive school environments.

REFERENCES

Ability Path. (2011). *Walk a mile in their shoes*. Retrieved from www.abilitypath.org

Anthamatten, E. (2014). What does it mean to 'Throw like a girl'? *The New York Times*. Retrieved from http://opinionator.blogs.nytimes.com/2014/08/24/what-does-it-mean-to-throw-like-a-girl/?_r=0

Baldry, A. (2005). Bystander behaviour among Italian students. *Pastoral Care in Education: An International Journal of Personal, Social and Emotional Development, 23*(2), 30–35. doi: 10.1111/j.0264-3944.2005.00329.x

Bawden, A. (2008, January 28). Sad to be gay: New guidance aims to end the rising tide of homophobic bullying-of pupils and teachers. *The Guardian*. Retrieved from http://www.theguardian.com/education/2008/jan/29/pupilbehaviour.schools

Boulton, M. J., & Smith, P. K. (1992). Ethnic preferences and perceptions among Asian and White British middle school children. *Social Development, 1*, 55–66. doi: 10.1111/j.1467-9507.1992.tb00134.x

Brinkman, B. G., Jedinak, A., Rosén, L. A., & Zimmerman, T. S. (2011). Teaching children fairness: Decreasing gender prejudice among children. *Analyses of Social Issues and Public Policy, 11*, 61–81. doi: 10.1111/j.1530-2415.2010.01222.x

Brinkman, B. G., & Manning, L. (in press). Children's intended responses to gender-based bullying as targets and bystanders. *Childhood*.

Brown, C. S., Alabi, B. O., Huynh, V. W., & Masten, C. L. (2011). Ethnicity and gender in late childhood and early adolescence: Group identity and awareness of bias. *Developmental Psychology, 47*(2), 463–471.

Brown, L. M. (2005). *Girlfighting: Betrayal and rejection among girls*. New York, NY: New York University Press.

Brown, L. M., Chesney-Lind, M., & Stein, N. (2007). Patriarchy matters: Toward a gendered theory of teen violence and victimization. *Violence Against Women, 13*, 1249–1273. doi: 10.1177/1077801207310430

Crick N. R., & Grotpeter J. K. (1995). Relational aggression, gender, and social-psychological adjustment. *Child Development, 66*, 710–722.

Crothers, L. M., Field, J. E., & Kolbert, J. B. (2005). Navigating power, control, and being nice: Aggression in adolescent girls' friendships. *Journal of Counseling and Development, 83*, 349–354. doi: 10.1002/j.1556-6678.2005.tb00354.x

Dewitt, P. (2012). *Dignity for all: Safeguarding LGBT students*. London, UK: Corwin.

Duncan, N. (1999). *Sexual bullying: Gender conflict and pupil culture in secondary schools*. London, England: Routledge.

Eder, D., Evans, C. C., & Stephen, P. (1995). *School talk: Gender and adolescent culture*. New Brunswick, NJ: Rutgers University Press.

Elze, D. E. (2003). Gay, lesbian, and bisexual youths perceptions of their high school environments and comfort in school. *Children & Schools, 25*, 225–239. doi: 10.1093/cs/25.4.225

Erikson, E. H. (1968). *Identity, youth and crisis*. New York, NY: Norton.

Eslea, M., & Mukhtar, K. (2000). Bullying and racism among Asian schoolchildren in Britain. *Educational Research, 42*, 207–217.

Espelage, D. L., & Swearer, S. M. (2004). *Bullying in American schools: A social-ecological perspective on prevention and intervention*. Mahwah, NJ: Lawrence Erlbaum Associates.

Espelage, D. L., & Swearer, S. M. (2008). Addressing research gaps in the intersection between homophobia and bullying. *School Psychology Review, 37*, 155–159.

Fried, S., & Soslan, B. (2011). *Banishing bullying behavior: Transforming the culture of peer abuse* (2nd ed.). Lanham, MD: Rowman & Littlefield Education.

Friedman, M. S., Koeske, G. F., Silvestre, A. J., Korr, W. S., & Sites, E. W. (2006). The impact of gender-role nonconforming behavior, bullying, and social support on suicidality among gay male youth. *Journal of Adolescent Health, 38*, 621–623.

Greytak, E. A., Kosciw, J. G., and Diaz, E. M. (2009). *Harsh realities: The experiences of transgender youth in our nation's schools*. New York: GLSEN.

Harber, C. (2009). *Toxic schooling: How schools became worse*. Nottingham, UK: Educational Heretics Press.

Heinze, J. E., & Horn, S. S. (2014). Do adolescents' evaluations of exclusion differ based on gender expression and sexual orientation? *Journal of Social Issues, 70*, 63–80.

Hinduja, S., & Patchin, J. W. (2012). *School climate 2.0: Preventing cyberbullying and sexting one classroom at a time.* Thousand Oaks, CA: Corwin.

Holcomb, S. (2011, December 3). Muslims in America: When bullying meets religion. *Muslim Matters.* Retrieved from http://muslimmatters.org/2011/12/13/muslims-in-america-when-bullying-meets-religion/

Huckstadt, L. K., & Shutts, K. (2014). How young children evaluate people with and without disabilities. *Journal of Social Issues, 70,* 99–114. doi: 10.1111/josi.12049

Jenkins, M. F., Zapf, D., Winefield, H., & Sarris, A. (2012). Bullying allegations from the accused bully's perspective. *British Journal of Management, 23,* 489–501. doi: 10.1111/j.1467-8551.2011.00778.x

Jenson, J. M., Dieterich, W. A., Brisson, D., Bender, K. A., & Powell, A. (2010). Preventing childhood bullying: Findings and lessons from the Denver public schools trial. *Research on Social Work Practice, 20,* 509–517.

Johnson, K. (2012, April 16). "Family: Bullies pushed NW Iowa teen to take own life". *KTIV.* Retrieved from http://www.ktiv.com/story/17473534/family-says

Katz, A., Buchanan, A., & Bream, V. (2001). *Bullying in Britain: Testimonies from teenagers.* London: Young Voice.

Katz, J., & Jhally, S. (1999, May 2). The national conversations in the wake of Littleton is missing the mark. *The Boston Globe.* Retrieved from http://www.jacksonkatz.com/pub_missing.html

Kimmel, M. (2009). *Guyland: The perilous world where boys become men.* New York, NY: Harper Collins Publishers.

Kimmel, M. S., & Mahler, M. (2003). Adolescent masculinity, homophobia, and violence: Random school shootings, 1982–2001. *American Behavioral Scientist, 46,* 1439–1458. doi: 10.1177/0002764203046010010

Klein, J. (2006). Cultural capital and high school bullies: How social inequality impacts school violence. *Men and Masculinities, 9,* 53–75. doi: 10.1177/1097184X04271387

Klein, J. (2012). *The bully society: School shootings and the crisis of bullying in America's schools.* New York, NY: New York University Press.

Kosciw, J. G., Greytak, E. A., Bartkiewicz, M., Boesen, M. J., & Palmer, N. A. (2012). *The 2011 national school climate survey: The experiences of lesbian, gay, bisexual, and transgender youth in our nation's schools.* New York: GLSEN.

Lamb, G. (2008, April 17). Columbine High School. *The New York Times.* Retrieved from http://topics.nytimes.com/top/reference/timestopics/organizations/c/columbine_high_school/index.html

Lamb, L. M., Bigler, R. S., Liben, L. S., & Green, V. A. (2009). Teaching children to confront peers' sexist remarks: Implications for theories of gender development and educational practice. *Sex Roles, 61,* 361–382.

Lamb, S. (2001). *The secret lives of girls: What good girls really do-sex play, aggression, and their guilt.* New York: The Free Press.

Liu, W. M., Soleck, G., Hopps, J., Dunston, K., & Pickett, T. (2004). A new framework to understand social class in counseling: The social class worldview and modern classism theory. *Journal of Multicultural Counseling and Development, 32,* 95–122. doi: 10.1002/j.2161-1912.2004.tb00364.x

Ma, X. (2001). Bullying and being bullied: To what extent are bullies also victims? *American Educational Research Journal, 38,* 351–570.

McGuire, J. K., Anderson, C. R., Toomey, R. B., & Russell, S. T. (2010). School climate for transgender youth: A mixed method investigation of student experiences and school responses. *Journal of Youth and Adolescence, 39,* 1175–1188.

McNamara, B. E. (2013). *Bullying and students with disabilities: Strategies and techniques to create a safe learning environment for all.* Thousand Oaks, CA: Corwin.

Meyer, E. J. (2009). *Gender, bullying, and harassment: Strategies to end sexism and homophobia in schools.* New York, NY: Teacher's College Press.

Mishna, F., Newman, P. A., Daley, A., & Solomon, S. (2009). Bullying of lesbian and gay youth: A qualitative investigation. *The British Journal of Social Work, 39,* 1598–1614.

Nansel, T., Overpeck, M., Pilla, R., Ruan, W., Simons-Morton, B., & Scheidt, P. (2001). Bullying behaviors among U.S. youth: Prevalence and association with psychosocial adjustment. *JAMA, 285,* 2094–2100.

Norwich, B., & Kelly, N. (2004). Pupils' views on inclusion: Moderate learning difficulties and bullying in mainstream and special schools. *British Educational Research Journal, 30,* 43–65. doi: 10.1080/0141192031001629965

O'Connell, P., Pepler, D., & Craig, W. (1999). Peer involvement in bullying: Insights and challenges for intervention. *Journal of Adolescence 22,* 437–452.

O'Connor, A. (2011, September, 21). Suicide draws attention to gay bullying. *The New York Times.* Retrieved from http://well.blogs.nytimes.com/2011/09/21/suicide-of-gay-teenager-who-urged-hope/?_r=0

Olweus, D. (1993). *Bullying at school: What we know and what we can do.* Oxford, UK: Blackwell.

Orpinas, P., & Horne, A. M. (2006). *Bullying prevention: Creating a positive school climate and developing social competencies.* Washington, DC: American Psychological Association.

Pascoe, C.J. (2007). *Dude, you're a fag: Masculinity and sexuality in high school.* Berkley, CA: University of California Press.

Pendragon, D. K. (2010). Coping behaviors among sexual minority female youth. *Journal of Lesbian Studies, 14,* 5–15.

Pollack, W. (1998) *Real boys: Rescuing our sons from the myths of boyhood.* Henry Hold and Company, NY: New York.

Poteat, V.P., & Espelage, D.L. (2005). Exploring the relation between bullying and homophobic verbal content: The homophobic content agent target (HCAT) scale. *Violence and Victims, 20,* 513–528.

Price, J. N. (1999). Schooling and racialized masculinities: The diploma, teachers, and peers in the lives of young, African American men. *Youth Society, 31,* 224–263.

Richardson, C. (2004, November 15). After school clubs: Queerbashing is a habit that is acquired in the playground but refined on the way home. *The Guardian.* Retrieved from http://www.theguardian.com/education/2004/nov/15/schools.uk

Rigby, K. (2004). Addressing bullying in schools: Theoretical perspectives and their implications. *School Psychology International, 25,* 287–300. doi: 10.1177/0143034304046902

Ringrose, J., & Renold, E. (2010). Normative cruelties and gender deviants: The performative effects of bully discourses for girls and boys in school. *British Educational Research Journal, 36,* 573–596.

Sellers, R. M., Copeland-Linder, N., Martin, P. P., & Lewis, R. L. (2006). Racial identity matters: The relationship between racial discrimination and psychological functioning in African American adolescents. *Journal of Research on Adolescence, 16,* 187–216. doi: 10.1111/j.1532-7795.2006.00128.x

Shepherd, S. (2011, March 10). White House conference tackles bullying. *CNN.* Retrieved from http://www.cnn.com/2011/POLITICS/03/10/obama.bullying/

Simons, R. L., Murry, V., McLoyd, V., Lin, K., Cutrona, C., & Conger, R. D. (2002). Discrimination, crime, ethnic identity, and parenting as correlates of depressive symptoms among African American children: A multilevel analysis. *Development and Psychopathology, 14,* 371–393.

Spurgeon, A. (1997). Commentary I. *Journal of Community & Applied Social Psychology, 7,* 240–244.

Strauss, S. (2012). *Sexual harassment and bullying: A guide to keeping kids safe and holding schools accountable.* Plymouth, UK: Rowman & Littlefield Publishers.

Stringer, M., Irwing, P., Giles, M., McClenahan, C., Wilson, R., & Hunter, J.A. (2009). Intergroup contact, friendship quality and political attitudes in integrated and segregated schools in Northern Ireland. *British Journal of Educational Psychology, 79,* 239–257. doi: 10.1348/978185408X368878

Swearer, S. M., Espelage, D. L., Vaillancourt, T., & Hymel, S. (2010). What can be done about school bullying? Linking research to educational practice. *Educational Researcher, 39,* 38–47. doi: 10.3102/0013189X09357622

Tanenbaum, L. (2000). *Slut! Growing up female with a bad reputation.* New York, NY: Harper Collins.

Taylor, C. R., & Stern, B. B. (1997). Asian-Americans: Television advertising and the 'model minority' stereotype. *Journal of Advertising, 26,* 47–61.

Tippett, N., Houlston, C., & Smith, P. K. (2010). *Prevention and response to identity-based bullying among local authorities in England, Scotland, and Wales* (Research report 64). London, England: Equality and Human Rights Commission.

Tolman, D. (2002). *Dilemmas of desire: Teenage girls talk about sexual desire.* Cambridge, MA: Harvard University Press.

Turner, K. L., & Brown, C. S. (2007). The centrality of gender and ethnic identities across individuals and contexts. *Social Development, 16,* 700–719. doi: 10.1111/j.1467-9507.2007.00403.x

Wessler, S. L., & De Andrade, L. L. (2006). Slurs, stereotypes, and student interventions: Examining the dynamics, impact, and prevention of harassment in middle and high school. *Journal of Social Issues, 62,* 511–532. doi: 10.1111/j.1540-4560.2006.00471.x

Wiseman, R. (2002). *Queen bees and wannabes.* New York, NY: Three Rivers Press.

Zhou, M., & Xiong, Y. S. (2005). The multifaceted American experiences of the children of the Asian immigrants: Lessons for segmented assimilation. *Ethnic and Racial Studies, 28,* 1119–1152.

Zimmerman, T. S., Aberle, J. M., & Krafchick, J. (2006). FAIR: A diversity and social justice curriculum for school counselors to integrate school-wide. *Guidance & Counselling, 1,* 47–56.

2 Examining Identity-Based Bullying as a Social Justice Issue

Dialogues and debates about the purpose of schooling often include conversations about what role (if any) schools should play in changing society. I assert that schools can and should become hubs for social justice work. In the current chapter, I argue that eradicating identity-based bullying is itself a social justice issue. I draw upon feminist scholarship and psychological research to examine the underlying and systemic causes of social injustice and to explore how scholars, educators, and practitioners can work toward the development of a more just society. In Chapter 5, I describe how policies and structures shape schooling and influence social justice programming. Here I demonstrate that many schools are structured in such a way that social inequalities are reproduced and reinforced. Examining identity-based bullying as a social justice issue requires us to: 1) recognize ways schools reinforce identity-based bullying and perpetuate social inequality, 2) identify the detrimental impact of identity-based bullying, and 3) explore the role schools can play in promoting justice and eradicating inequity.

WHAT IS SOCIAL JUSTICE?

It is important to note that there are multiple ways to understand the term *social justice*. Various scholars have offered definitions for the terms *justice*—each with different implications. Bell (2007) defines social justice as "a vision of society in which the distribution of resources is equitable and all members are physically and psychologically safe and secure" (p. 1). Although definitions vary, many individuals utilize the term social justice to indicate the pursuit of equality. Some have interpreted equality to mean pursuing sameness or uniformity in all areas. By contrast, I conceptualize social justice as the pursuit of *complex equality*, which recognizes that not all situations are the same, nor are all people's needs uniform (Connell, 2005). The quest for such complex equality in the name of social justice requires identifying the systems in which some individuals are given resources and power over others and changing the structures that allow such inequity to exist and persist. Vera, Buhin, and Isacco (2009) assert that unjust processes will always result in unjust outcomes; and as such, an equal distribution of resources within a society will never be achieved unless people address and change the underlying causes of inequity. In this book, I draw upon two particular bodies of work to inform my perspective of social justice. The first includes feminist literature—an interdisciplinary body of work informed by a shared movement(s) and common goals. In particular, I utilize feminist work that emphasizes intersections of identity, challenges patriarchal systems, and prioritizes human dignity and justice for all. As a counseling psychologist, I am also informed by work within psychology that emphasizes multicultural competence, advocacy, and activism work.

Patriarchy and Inequality

A social justice perspective regarding identity-based bullying calls for exploring the deeper and systemic causes of identity-based bullying rather than viewing it as a product of individual pathology or interpersonal conflict. Within this book, I draw upon feminist scholarship to conceptualize the etiology of injustice and to inform the understanding of identity-based bullying as a product of an unjust society.

Feminist perspectives of social justice explore how power is distributed, utilized, and reinforced within patriarchal systems. *Patriarchy* is most simply defined as a system in which power is given to men (as a group) over women (as a group) (Newman, 2011). Such patriarchal societies (including the United States of America and the United Kingdom) function as hierarchies and fail to distribute power and access to resources in a just manner. Resources are not distributed by population density; instead, people higher up in the hierarchy are given more access to resources than people lower in the hierarchy. Within patriarchal systems, men as a group are given more power than women, but other aspects of identity are important as well in determining where a particular individual falls in the hierarchy. Within the U.S. and the U.K., other areas of identity that may influence one's position in the system include: race/ethnicity/nationality, gender expression, sexual orientation, social class, religion, and ability status. *Resources* include all those things (tangible and intangible) that are considered valuable within a society. This includes money and other material goods, as well as access to decision-making power, education, prestige, and privilege.

Privilege is a type of resource that is often invisible to those who have it and is sometimes hard to pinpoint by those who do not have it. Privilege includes both unearned entitlements (things that all people should have, such as safety) and conferred dominance (something that gives one person power over others) (McIntosh, 2004). For example, feeling generally safe to walk down the street alone without fear of being catcalled or experiencing sexual violence is a privilege held by most (heterosexual) men but not women. Similarly, within the U.S. and the U.K., the ability to publicly display affection toward one's intimate partner without fear of being harassed or assaulted is a privilege held by most heterosexuals but not same-sex couples. Privilege also applies to children's experiences in schools. Learning about individuals who share one's identity is a privilege experienced by White students, as most history books used in schools in the U.S. feature White individuals more than people of color. As a result, White students may differ from African American students in their explanations of important themes in U.S. history and may feel less connected to historical events (Epstein, 1998).

This description of patriarchy is certainly an imperfect and overly simplistic representation of a very complex system. One important point to note is that in most patriarchal societies there is not an even rate of change of resources within the hierarchy. In fact, in most patriarchal societies, wealth it is not distributed equally, nor does it increase at a steady pace. One report of wealth inequality in the U.S. showed that in 2007, the top 1% of the country owned 34.6% of the wealth, while the bottom 40% owned just 0.2% (Wolff, 2010). It is also important to point out that people do not consist of just one identity, thus finding any one individual's place within the system can be tricky. For example, a working class, gay, White man in the United States may have access to resources and privilege by nature of his gender and ethnicity but may be denied resources and privileges as a result of his sexual orientation and social class.

Upward Mobility and Changing Identities

Individuals may be able to change their position in the system during their lifetime. Within the U.S., the possibility of upward mobility is commonly held as a core value (Du Bois, 1995), but the reality of such movement is far less likely than the American mythos would lead one to believe. Some children find that education, hard work, and luck allow them to have greater access to resources than their parents had. However, the opportunities for upward mobility may be particularly lacking for individuals from marginalized groups, especially African Americans (Cole & Omari, 2003). Hill and Torres (2010) found that many U.S. Latinos are struggling to move up the social ladder, despite valuing education and having parental support for upward mobility. In England, there are numerous barriers and complications to upward mobility. For example, the ability for parents to engage in and support their children's educational efforts may depend to some extent on their own educational experiences, which often vary by social class backgrounds. One area where the gap between parents from various backgrounds may be growing involves the use of and access to technology (Hollingworth, Mansaray, Allen, & Rose, 2011). Despite continued belief in the possibility, in both the U.S. and the U.K., there are multiple barriers to the reality of upward mobility.

Societies can (and do) change over time in the way resources are distributed. First, the amount of resources that those at the top hold compared to those at the bottom can change. This shift has been seen within the United States over the past half of a century, especially as it relates to monetary resources. In 2013, an average CEO in the U.S. made 296 times the average wage of a worker (Hiscott, 2014). Many estimates suggest that in the 1950s, the CEO-to-worker wage gap was just 20–1 (Smith & Kuntz, 2013). Societies also change in regard to which aspects of identity result in individuals receiving more or less institutional power. For example, Roediger (2007) argues that the creation of *whiteness* in the United States emerged as part of a class versus ethnicity battle that drew lines between Irish immigrants and African Americans. When Irish immigrants came to the U.S. in large numbers in the 1800s, they were considered by many to be unwanted minorities— many faced employment and interpersonal discrimination. However, as the U.S. focused more on the creation of whiteness as an identity in order to justify an unequal distribution of power, Irish individuals and those of Irish decent were included in this new demographic (Roediger, 2007). Now, despite challenges they faced in the past, in most of America, those who are of Irish decent are considered White. Many U.S. cities hold large St. Patrick's Day parades and celebrate all things Irish (and faux Irish). Despite the potential for change within these systems, ultimately the patriarchal structure is defined by limiting access to resources to some people over others.

Social Justice as a Means for Change

Feminist scholars have articulated the problems related to an unjust society and proposed ways to create social change. In particular, social justice emerges as a counter to patriarchal systems where resources are not justly or fairly distributed within a population. bell hooks (1996) articulates that social justice efforts can (and should) work simultaneously to change individuals as well as social systems and structures, "There must exist a paradigm, a practical model for social change that includes an understanding of ways to transform consciousness that are linked to efforts to transform structures" (p. 193). Feminist perspectives about the best means of achieving social justice vary. Some feminist approaches advocate for changes in policies and laws to ensure more equitable access to resources, while others believe that a larger shift in the structure of society is needed to achieve social justice. Feminist viewpoints about social justice are often integrated into the work of individuals in various disciplines (including psychology and education) and help to inform how practitioners within those disciplines conceptualize and give voice to a social justice agenda.

Although perhaps not always a focal point within psychology, many professional organizations that psychologists and school counselors belong to have advocated for social justice. The American Psychological Association releases various reports regarding effective ways to address identity issues within research and clinical work. This has often taken the form of reports focused on specific social issues or aspects of identity (e.g., *Guidelines for*

Psychological Practice with Girls and Women, 2007). Psychologists who do applied work in the form of therapy, programming, and consultation are expected to be multiculturally competent. Specifically, the profession's ethical code stipulates the necessity of being competent to work with clients from diverse backgrounds and with various social identities, and it explicitly notes the expectation that professionals value the dignity of all people (American Psychological Association, 2010). Some scholars have called for psychologists and other mental health professionals to take a more active role in advocating for social change, going beyond basic research about diversity issues. For example, the Transforming School Counseling Initiative (Erford, House, & Martin, 2007) calls for school counselors to play an active role in transforming school climates into spaces that are just and equitable. Similarly, the National Association of School Psychologists (NASP, 2011) published a position paper regarding LGBT youth in which they outline the role of the school psychologist as both supporting individual LGBT students and advocating for their rights and respect within school systems. Psychologists and other mental health professionals can use their expertise to work toward bettering the lives of all people by combating oppression and inequality.

The Society for the Psychological Study of Social Issues (SPSSI; Division 9 of the American Psychological Association) has a long history of advocating for social justice. SPSSI was founded by social psychologists who were concerned that research being done within the discipline remained too entrenched in the academy and was not being utilized to support social change. SPSSI has a mission to apply "research on the psychological aspects of important social issues to public policy solutions" (SPSSI, n.d.). The Society of Counseling Psychology (SCP; Division 17 of the American Psychological Association) also encourages psychologists to integrate social justice approaches into their work not only by supporting clients who are facing the negative repercussions of inequality and oppression but also by taking an active role in advocating for system changes through prevention and policy work (Kenny, Horne, Orpinas & Reese, 2009; Toporek, Gerstein, Foud, Roysircar, & Israel, 2006). The Association for Women in Psychology, founded in 1969, is "committed to a just and inclusive world without sexism and oppression, one that supports the psychological development and well-being of all people" (AWP, n.d.). The organization supports feminist scholarship and practice and promotes social justice.

REPRODUCTION OF INEQUALITY WITHIN SCHOOLS

A number of scholars within the United States and United Kingdom (as well as other nations) have examined the role of schooling within society. Many of these scholars have critiqued the ways that schools reproduce inequality and teach children about the "accepted" social order (Freire, 1970; Harber,

2009; Illich, 1971; Jackson, 1968). The individuals making decisions about policies and curriculum in schools are almost always those from dominant groups, so they (intentionally or unintentionally) develop systems that continue to support mainstream students (often White, heterosexual, middle class) even to the detriment of others (Harber, 2009). Freire (1970) articulated the belief that educational systems that utilize a "banking" model (in which teachers "deposit" education into receptive students) create oppressive structures in which teachers exert power over children. This approach to education teaches children that society functions in a similar way—that some people hold power over others. If the curriculum is designed to reinforce and support the current social structure, it is unlikely that educators will emphasize being flexible, envisioning a new future, or working to change the social order. Instead, schools generally encourage students to develop a uniform worldview without many alternatives.

Schools often try to reach students in the midrange; brighter students and students who struggle with the material may feel left out (Harber, 2009). Similarly, many of the social policies seek to support "typical" (or at least the adults' ideas about typicality) students. Students who are not typical because they do not conform to stereotypical gender roles, have religious or cultural values that differ from the majority of students in the school, or have different abilities than others and may find themselves without much support. As a result of reinforcing dominate social structures, many schools play a role in creating prejudice by socializing students and indoctrinating them into beliefs about group identities and stereotypes (Harber, 2009). One way that inequality is reproduced within schools occurs when students engage in identity-based bullying in their attempts to enforce such beliefs.

Schools often reinforce gender inequities and stereotypes related to gender identity. Most schools are more gender segregated than other areas of a student's life. In fact, schools often go out of their way to separate boys and girls and use institutional and language-based gender practices to create and recreate inequality (Eder, Evans, & Stephen, 1995). Boys are given more attention, called on more frequently, provided more encouragement, and given more resources for their activities (particularly sports) (Strauss, 2012). Girls are encouraged to defer to boys, are often praised for their appearance and neatness, and given less support for their interest in nontraditional fields. In many schools, the social traditions as well as classroom exercises reflect stereotypical attitudes about gender roles. For example, in her book detailing an in-depth study of masculinity and sexuality within an American high school, Pascoe (2007) describes an annual assembly whose purpose was to crown the most popular senior boy as "Mr. Cougar." During the assembly, candidates performed skits in an attempt to win votes from the students. Pascoe describes how this competition highlighted core tenants of hegemonic masculinity, including hyper-heterosexuality, physical prowess, competitiveness, and antifemininity. These types of ceremonies and traditions, along with many school structures, are designed to separate genders and encourage false distinctions, making the space challenging for children who do not conform to gender-role stereotypes. In these ways, schools create a climate that encourages conformity to traditional gender norms, supports heterosexual relationships, and defines the invisible norms of the school (and arguably, teach children that these are the norms of society).

Recent studies of schools in Great Britain have demonstrated ways that schools reproduce and maintain social and economic inequalities (Asthana & Hinsliff, 2006; Taylor, 2006). Children from poor families often fall behind students from rich families, because the wealthier students have access to resources and opportunities outside of school that the poorer children do not have. Today, kids from poor and/or minority communities continue to have the most limited options for education and the bleakest outcomes. In the U.S., high school graduation rates highlight inequalities being reproduced within the school system. As of 2010, 51% of African American students graduated high school, compared to 55% of Latinos and 76% of Whites (Weber, 2010).

Educational inequality based on race or economic status is certainly not a new phenomenon in the United States. In many ways, such disparities were codified into the educational system with segregation and a system of funding schools through local taxes (see chapter 5 for a discussion of the structure of schooling in the U.S. and the U.K.). The landmark decision in the *Brown v. Board of Education* Supreme Court case (1954) was based on research demonstrating that separate schools were NOT equal. Thurgood Marshall presented the findings from a set of research studies indicating that Black and White children preferred White dolls and endorsed a range of positive traits for White dolls, while indicating that the Black dolls likely had negative characteristics (Clark & Clark, 1939, 1947). Marshall argued that this research was evidence that the *separate but equal* policy was actually doing harm to Black children by negatively impacting their self-image (Woo, 2005). Civil Rights leaders asserted segregated schools were a training ground for a segregated society that ensured resources provided to the "haves" stayed in their hands, while continuing to cripple the ability of the "have nots" to rise above. Longitudinal research examining the time following the *Brown v. Board of Education* decision demonstrated that numerous benefits resulted from desegregation (Pettigrew, 2004). Much improvement occurred starting in the 1950s; unfortunately, this period of change became stagnant in the 1970s (Weber, 2010).

Today, few Americans recognize the continued inequities within the educational system or do not see them as a social justice issue demanding resolution. Many Americans with the means to do so choose to send their children to private or charter schools. According to the National Center for Education Statistics, during the 2011–2012 school year, 10% of American children attended private schools and 4.2% of children who attended public schools went to charter schools. While these parents may be concerned about the state of the local public schools, they understandably use every resource they have to give their children the best education possible. Sadly, this means that those without the time/money/political power to send their children to a private school, get them into a charter school, or homeschool them are left to hope that their children get a quality education within the public system.

Identity-Based Bullying is a Mechanism of Creating and Reinforcing Inequality

Identity-based bullying in schools is one way that inequality is created and reinforced. Students recreate power plays they witness taking place between adults, internalize stereotypes about various aspects of identities, and discriminate against others through identity-based bullying. In Chapter 3, I describe this development of discrimination within children and the manifestation of identity-based bullying. Here I argue that identity-based bullying functions within the school system to perpetuate social injustices.

If school systems function in such a way that some groups of people have power over others, students will learn to look for ways their identity can provide them with access to that power. Identity-based bullying can both reflect the state of a school and impact the school by reinforcing a "culture of hierarchy through dominance and aggression" (Strauss, 2012, p. 58). If identity-based bullying is dismissed by teachers and administrators, this sends a message to children about who "belongs" in the space and who is valued. For example, schools in which sexual harassment occurs regularly and is dismissed as "normal" male behavior may foster environments in which girls do not feel safe. These schools may also encourage climates in which harassment escalates into physical violence, including sexual assault. In some schools, students who engage in bullying (whether it is identity-based or not) do not face disciplinary practices if they are well liked by the teachers or belong to privileged groups. Some scholars have examined ways in which male members of sports teams may be given a pass when they engage in violent or harassing behaviors because of their status within the school (Kimmel, 2009). There are often differences in the disciplinary practices of teachers and school administrators based on the race of the student (Gregory, 1995), and students notice these differences. Such discrepancies send a message to students about the attitude the school has about how to treat others and reinforces inequalities.

Identity-based bullying is different from other types of bullying given that individuals are targeted because of some aspect of their social identity, such as their race/ethnicity, social class, gender, etc. As a result, those who share an identity with victims are impacted by bullying, even in cases where they are not being directly targeted. Chesir-Teran and Hughes (2009) describe the vicarious victimization of some LGB students. Even those students who reported that they experienced little direct harassment indicated that they were aware of the bullying that was occurring against other LGB students and the ways in which it was often tolerated by teachers and school officials. In this way, identity-based bullying is shaped by and shapes the social environment within a school.

Some students who have been victimized by identity-based bullying or who fear the potential of becoming a victim may actually perpetuate inequalities within schools by engaging in such behaviors themselves. Some boys report that they think they are doing a helpful thing when they tease another boy about his masculinity presentation (Duncan, 1999). They believe that they are helping to shape their peers to conform to society's expectations for them. When school structures reinforce the idea that resources (including dignity, respect) are limited, students may decide that their best option is to compete with each other for status and power. A social justice perspective that emphasizes system change will help to better understand, and hopefully break, this cycle of identity-based bullying.

IMPACT OF IDENTITY-BASED BULLYING

As noted, the pursuit of social justice is not about ensuring that everyone is treated in the exact same way, rather the goal is to challenge structures that result in inequitable outcomes and to ensure that all individuals are physically and psychologically safe. Research within psychology has illuminated the many ways that people's physical and emotional well-being are harmed by oppression, stereotypes, and discrimination. Most of this research has been conducted with adults and has examined the effects of everyday discrimination, as well as the impact of institutionalized oppression. Research on the impact of discrimination on children (although less of it has been conducted than research with adults) has similarly found harmful effects. Students who experience identity-based bullying may be subjected to a wide range of negative consequences.

Some scholars have argued that racial discrimination is a type of chronic stress in the lives of children of color and that these experiences can have numerous negative impacts on the physical and mental well-being of children (Sanders-Phillips, 2009). For example, a longitudinal study of the impact of discrimination on African American adolescents indicated that those who reported more experiences of discrimination had more potentially self-destructive cognitions and engaged in more self-destructive behaviors (such as risky sex) than those who reported fewer discrimination experiences (Gibbons et al., 2012). Children who experience racial discrimination may have lowered self-esteem and increased rates of depression (Greene, Way, & Pahl, 2006). African American adolescents' experiences of discrimination are associated with lower psychological well-being and higher stress and depressive symptoms (Sellers, Copeland-Linder, Martin, &

Lewis, 2006). One longitudinal study found a relationship between the discrimination African American students experienced in high school and lower self-esteem, less belief in their competency, less motivation to achieve, and lower levels of resiliency (Wong, Eccles, & Sameroff, 2003). Further, racial discrimination within school settings has been shown to be associated with depressive symptoms for ethnic minority immigrant children in the U.S. (Tummala-Narra & Claudius, 2013).

Other forms of identity-based bullying may also result in detrimental physical and psychological outcomes for the targets and others in the school. Children who experience sexual harassment have reported numerous negative symptoms, including feeling nervous and sad, loss of appetite, loss of interest in activities, nightmares, lowered self-esteem, and tardiness in school. Most studies suggest that girls experience more of these effects than do boys, even when boys experience some sexual harassment (Strauss, 2012). Bullying about masculinity that emphasizes heterosexuality and sexual "conquests" has implications for girls and boys (and later, women and men) throughout society. Boys may avoid being emotionally expressive or affectionate with girlfriends and may be encouraged to talk about sex and demonstrate their desire for sex to their friends. Boys may engage in sexual harassment of girls in order to display their sexual prowess. Some adolescent boys may go to extreme lengths to avoid being teased about sexual inexperience, including going to a prostitute or even drugging and sexually assaulting young women (Pascoe, 2007). Youth who have experienced identity-based bullying report feeling like they are less valued and their lives are less important. One LGB young adult spoke about the result of experiencing bullying in schools as an adolescent. "You would begin to feel that you weren't worth being protected if you weren't protected by your school or your parents or the other kids. You would begin to feel that being different was bad" (Mishna et al., 2009, p. 1604). Questioning whether one belongs or is valued within a school can result in numerous negative consequences. For example, Fletcher (2011) demonstrated that college enrollment rates are related to the extent to which adolescents feel that they belong in their school environment.

Klein (2012) also argues that many of the incidents of school shootings that have taken place within the United States in the past few decades can be understood as one of the most severe outcomes of identity-based bullying. According to some reports, 75% of school shootings are connected to bullying or harassment of the shooters (Groundspark, 2009). Most of the shootings were perpetrated by young men who had been bullied at school for not being "masculine" enough. These boys sought revenge for the bullying they experienced through what could be considered hyper-masculine methods, including violence using guns (Klein, 2012). These boys often targeted the students who bullied them or girls who rejected them. Obviously, not all boys who are bullied for their perceived lack of conformity to masculinity norms will retaliate with violence, and it is essential for psychologists and educators to continue to understand why some do, in order to find effective ways of preventing such heinous crimes. As educators, scholars, and parents who are concerned with the safety of children in schools, we should examine messages that reinforce traditional masculinity, including those that glorify violence.

Some studies have shown that identity-based bullying may have more negative impacts on a child than other forms of bullying. One study found that boys who experienced gender-based bullying (especially being called *gay*) reported greater distress and more negative perceptions of school than boys who were bullied for other reasons (Swearer, Turner, Givens, & Pollack, 2008). The negative effects of identity-based bullying can be long term. LGBT young adults who experienced high levels of identity-based bullying and victimization during adolescence were 2.6 times more likely to report clinical depression and 5.6 times more likely to report having attempted suicide when compared to their peers who reported low levels of victimization (Russell, Ryan, Toomey, Diaz, & Sanchez, 2011).

POTENTIAL FOR SCHOOLS TO SUPPORT SOCIAL JUSTICE

Schools often emphasize their responsibility to educate children about important content areas they need for day-to-day life (such as math, science, writing), but it is important not to forget the role that schools have in teaching children about being members of a diverse society. The experiences that kids have in school can have profound effects on their development as socially responsible citizens (Smith, 2012). What students see and experience during their time at school can influence how they think about fairness, justice, and morality. Addressing identity-based bullying as a social justice issue allows educators to see the bigger picture and wider impact of their work.

Moving Beyond Neutrality

In the United States, some schools have adopted *value neutral* policies regarding sexual orientation, which many teachers have argued serve as a "gag order" against discussing LGBTQ students or issues (Bazelon, 2012). Schools may utilize such a neutral approach to diversity issues as a way to avoid controversy, often arguing that these guidelines allow all perspectives to be equally valued. In practice, such policies serve to support those who are members of the privileged identity—often at the expense of others. A neutral approach to sexual orientation within a culture where heterosexuality is considered the "norm" can result in the dismissing of homosexuality at best and outright discrimination and hostility at worst. One teacher at a U.S. school that recently lost a court case about its neutrality policy said, "This policy clearly sends a message to LGBT kids that there is something shameful about who they are and that they are not valid people in history" (Eckholm, 2011). Even if schools do not think they are explicitly advocating a heterosexual norm, often the hidden curriculum within schools does just that. One British scholar who examined the English National Curriculum found that patterns of language reflected a discourse of heterosexism and a lack of awareness of sexual diversity (Sauntson, 2013). In reality, a neutral approach does not exist; a system can either support the status quo and thus those who already have privilege, or work to challenge it.

Value neutral policies endorse attitudes that parallel *colorblindness*, a "racial ideology that posits the best way to end discrimination is by treating individuals as equally as possible, without regard to race, culture, or ethnicity" (Williams, 2011). While individuals and schools may adopt colorblindness with good intentions, this approach serves to reinforce racism rather than end it. The basic premise is that all people are alike inside, thus race/ethnicity is not important. This belief invalidates the ways in which racial and ethnic identity contribute to children's identities. A colorblind approach also invalidates children's experiences of racism. It neglects to address the ways in which social structures have not been colorblind and the fact that these systems can shape and influence the experiences of marginalized groups. For groups who have been negatively affected by these structures, they cannot simply ignore the presence of race and racism. This ideology also supports the invisible norm of whiteness. Grimes (2002) argues that whiteness is often masked or actively ignored in such a way that whiteness is deemed the invisible norm. Within the USA, this norm is manifested in the ways that White/European Americans often see themselves. When asked to talk about their experiences of their own ethnicity, White Americans often articulate whiteness as being assumed or normalized (Frankenberg, 1993) or as representing a universal "insider" (Jackson, 1999). Individuals who endorse a colorblind ideology may deny institutional racism and the existence of White privilege (Neville, Awad, Brooks, Flores, & Bluemel, 2013). Endorsing a colorblind ideology may also lead one to engage in more instances of microaggressions when compared to individuals who do not endorse this way of thinking. Microaggressions can include microassaults, microinsults, and microinvalidations, which have a negative impact on targets, even if perpetrators are unaware that they are committing them (Sue et al., 2007).

School systems that rely on a colorblind ideology in the way they develop policies and practices often create environments that are hostile to students of color (Chapman, 2013). For example, in 2013, Arizona's department of education objected to the Tucson School District's course on multicultural literature, saying it would violate a law that prohibits any courses that encourage "ethnic solidarity" (Planas, 2013). In some ways, this law attempted to codify schools' use of a colorblind ideology, stressing that all pupils should be treated as individuals. While reliance on a colorblind approach to address (or more accurately, ignore) racial issues within schools is not new, the approach was actually accentuated in some American communities following the election of President Obama in 2008 (Aleman, Salazar, Rorrer, & Parker, 2011). Some argued that the election of a Black president signaled that the U.S. had entered a post-racial era where issues of race and ethnicity no longer needed attention. However, school systems continue to engage in practices that are inequitable (Aleman et al., 2011), and the belief that racism is a thing of the past is detrimental when it allows schools to ignore inequalities within their own systems.

Rethinking the Role of Schools

Schools can be spaces that teach children alternatives to societal messages that reinforce inequality and stereotypes about social identities. For example, Klein (2012) argues that schools can provide young men with an alternative definition of masculinity, one that does not emphasize the use of violence to solve problems. Schools can teach children critical thinking skills and the ability to talk about controversial issues, and they can educate them against intolerance (Davies, 2008). Education can be a tool to prepare students to live in a democratic society in which all individuals are respected and individual differences are celebrated for adding diversity of perspectives and values to the whole group. An antiracist and social justice perspective in education creates a framework for doing this.

Banks (1993) describes the need to reform educational institutions so that students of all racial, ethnic, and social class groups (to which I would add sexual orientations and ability status) and male and female students experience educational equality. He proposes Five Key Dimensions of Multicultural Education (see Banks, 1993 for review of literature in each of these areas):

1. Content integration: using examples, data, and sources of information from a variety of cultural groups and perspectives
2. The knowledge construction process: helping students understand how knowledge is created and who has played a role in creating the knowledge
3. Prejudice reduction: helping children develop equitable attitudes and reduce their engagement in prejudice
4. Equity pedagogy: using a variety of pedagogical approaches so as to facilitate learning by all students
5. Empowering school culture: reforming institutionalized factors of the school environment and culture to reflect the needs and experiences of all students

Many schools only consider multicultural education to encompass curriculum reform (if they consider it at all) so that the content reflects material representing a broader range of people (including women and people of color). However, educational scholars (such as Alexander, 2001; Banks,

1993, 2006) argue that true multicultural education requires structural reforms of school policies and procedures. True reform addresses the teaching style as well as content; challenges stereotypes that teachers or administrators hold about people from various identities; and addresses how the social norms within a school may lead to privilege and oppression of marginalized groups. While these attempts to make institutional changes can be challenging and met with resistance, a social justice perspective to understanding and stopping identity-based bullying requires advocating for new priorities within education.

CONCLUSION

Identity-based bullying is a societal problem, and the most effective prevention and intervention strategies extend beyond changing any one individual (or a series of individuals). Identity-based bullying thrives within social structures that support and reinforce inequity. All too often, schools are exemplars of such a social system—one in which power and resources are not equitably distributed and students compete against each other for access. However, if societies shift the role of education toward promoting social justice, we can explore new possibilities about how to approach schooling. As educators, scholars, and mental health professionals, I believe we have a responsibility to embrace such possibilities, because all children deserve to attend schools that provide safe, supportive environments that reinforce equity and teach respect for all people.

REFERENCES

Aleman, E., Salazar, T., Rorrer, A., & Parker, L. (2011). Introduction to postracialism in U.S. public school and higher education settings: The politics of education in the age of Obama. *Peabody Journal of Education, 86,* 479–487.

Alexander, R.J. (2001). *Culture and pedagogy: International comparisons in primary education.* Oxford: Blackwell Publishing.

American Psychological Association. (2010, February 20). *Ethical principles of psychologists and code of conduct.* Retrieved from http://www.apa.org/ethics/code/principles.pdf

Asthana, A., & Hinsliff, G. (2006, February 4). How poor children miss out on the best schools. *The Guardian.* Retrieved from http://www.theguardian.com/uk/2006/feb/05/politics.schools

AWP Mission statement. (n.d.). Retrieved from http://www.awpsych.org/

Banks, J. (1993). Multicultural education: Historical development, dimensions, and practice. *Review of Research in Education, 19,* 3–49.

Banks, J. (2006). *Cultural diversity and education: Foundations, curriculum, and teaching* (5th ed.). Boston, MA: Pearson Education.

Bazelon, E. (2012, March 7). A big win: The landmark settlement in a Minnesota bullying case and how it could help gay students everywhere. *Slate.* Retrieved

from http://www.slate.com/articles/news_and_politics/bulle/2012/03/the_anoka_hennepin_settlement_a_big_win_in_the_fight_against_gay_bashing_bullies_.html
Bell, L. A. (2007). Theoretical foundations for social justice education. In M. Adams, L. A. Bell, & P. Griffin (Eds.), *Teaching for diversity and social justice* (2nd ed., pp. 3–16). New York, NY: Routledge.
Chapman, T. K. (2013). You can't erase race! Using CRT to explain the presence of race and racism in majority white suburban schools. *Discourse: Studies in the Cultural Politics of Education, 34*, 611–627.
Chesir-Teran, D., & Hughes, D. (2009). Heterosexism in high school and victimization among lesbian, gay, bisexual and questioning youth. *Journal of Youth and Adolescence, 38*, 963–975. doi: 10.1007/s10964-008-9364-x
Clark, K. B., & Clark, M. K. (1939). Segregation as a factor in the racial identification of Negro pre-school children: A preliminary report. *The Journal of Experimental Education, 8*, 161–163.
Clark, K. B., & Clark, M. K. (1947). Racial identification and preference in Negro children. In T. N. Newcomb & E. L. Hartley (Eds.), *Readings in social psychology* (pp. 551–560). New York, NY: Henry Holt.
Cole, E. R., & Omari, S. R. (2003). Race, class and the dilemmas of upward mobility for African Americans. *Journal of Social Issues, 59*(4), 785–802. doi: 10.1046/j.0022-4537.2003.00090.x
Connell, R. W. (2005). *Masculinities.* Los Angeles, CA: University of California Press.
Davies, L. (2008). *Educating against extremism.* Stoke on Trent, UK: Trentham Books.
Du Bois, C. (1995). The dominant value profile of American culture. *American Anthropologist, 57*, 1232–1239.
Duncan, N. (1999). *Sexual bullying: Gender conflict and pupil culture in secondary schools.* London, England: Routledge.
Eckholm, E. (2011, September 13). In suburb, battle goes public on bullying of gay students. *The New York Times.* Retrieved from http://www.nytimes.com/2011/09/13/us/13bully.html?ref=us&pagewanted=print&_r=0
Eder, D., Evans, C. C., & Stephen, P. (1995). *School talk: Gender and adolescent culture.* New Brunswick, NJ: Rutgers University Press.
Epstein, T. (1998). Deconstructing differences in African-American and European American adolescents' perspectives on US history. *Curriculum Inquiry, 28*, 397–423.
Erford, B. T., House, R. M., & Martin, P. (2007). Transforming the school counseling profession. In B. T. Erford (Ed.), *Transforming the school counseling profession* (2nd ed., pp. 1–12). Columbus, OH: Pearson Merrill Prentice Hall.
Fletcher, J. M. (2011). Social identity as a determinant of college enrollment. *Rationality and Society, 23*, 267–303. doi: 10.1177/1043463111404666
Frankenberg, R. (1993). *White women, race matters: The social construction of whiteness.* Minneapolis, MN: University of Minnesota Press.
Freire, P. (1970). *Pedagogy of the oppressed.* New York, NY: The Continuum International Publishing Group.
Gibbons, F. X., Roberts, M. E., Gerrard, M., Li, Z., Beach, S. R. H., Simons, R. L., & Philibert, R. A. (2012). The impact of stress on the life history strategies of African American adolescents: Cognitions, genetic moderation, and the role of discrimination. *Developmental Psychology, 48*, 722–739.
Greene, M. L., Way, N., & Pahl, K. (2006). Trajectories of perceived adult and peer discrimination among Black, Latino, and Asian American adolescents: Patterns and psychological correlates. *Developmental Psychology, 42*, 218–236. Retrieved from http://dx.doi.org/10.1037/0012-1649.42.2.218
Gregory, J. F. (1995). The crime of punishment: Racial and gender disparities in the use of corporal punishment in U.S. public schools. *Journal of Negro Education, 64*, 454–463.

Grimes, D. S. (2002). Challenging the status quo? Whiteness in the diversity management literature. *Management Communication Quarterly, 15,* 381–409. doi: 10.1177/0893318902153003

Groundspark. (2009). *Bullying and school climate statistics.* Retrieved from http://groundspark.org/our-films-and-campaigns/lets-get-real/lgr_stats

Harber, C. (2009). *Toxic schooling: How schools became worse.* Nottingham, UK: Educational Heretics Press.

Hill, N. E., & Torres, K. (2010). Negotiating the American dream: The paradox of aspirations and achievement among Latino students and engagement between their families and schools. *Journal of Social Issues, 66,* 95–112.

Hiscott, R. (2014, June 12). CEO pay has increased by 937 percent since 1978. *The Huffington Post.* Retrieved from http://www.huffingtonpost.com/2014/06/12/ceo-pay-report_n_5484622.html

Hollingworth, S., Mansaray, A., Allen, K., & Rose, A. (2011). Parents' perspectives on technology and children's learning in the home: Social class and the role of the habitus. *Journal of Computer Assisted Learning, 27,* 347–360. doi: 10.1111/j.1365-2729.2011.00431.x

hooks, b. (1996). *Killing rage: Ending racism.* New York, NY: Henry Holt and Company.

Illich, I. (1971). *Deschooling society.* New York, NY: Marion Boyars Publishers.

Jackson, P. W. (1968). *Life in classrooms.* New York, NY: Teacher's College Press.

Jackson, R. L., II. (1999). White space, white privilege: Mapping discursive inquiry into the self. *Quarterly Journal of Speech, 85,* 38–54.

Kenny, M. E., Horne, A. M., Orpinas, P., & Reese, L. E. (Eds.). (2009). *Realizing social justice: The challenge of preventive interventions.* Washington, DC: American Psychological Association.

Kimmel, M. (2009). *Guyland: The perilous world where boys become men.* New York, NY: Harper Collins Publishers.

Klein, J. (2012). *The bully society: School shootings and the crisis of bullying in America's schools.* New York, NY: New York University Press.

McIntosh, P. (2004). White privilege: Unpacking the invisible knapsack. In P. S. Rothenberg (Ed.), *Race, class and gender in the United States* (6th ed., pp. 97–101). New York, NY: Worth Publishers.

Mishna, F., Newman, P. A., Daley, A., & Solomon, S. (2009). Bullying of lesbian and gay youth: A qualitative investigation. *The British Journal of Social Work, 39,* 1598–1614.

National Association of School Psychologists. (2011, July 16). *Lesbian, gay, bisexual, transgender and questioning youth: Position statement.* Retrieved from http://www.nasponline.org/about_nasp/positionpapers/LGBTQ_Youth.pdf

Neville, H. A., Awad, G. H., Brooks, J. E., Flores, M. P., & Bluemel, J. (2013). Color-blind racial ideology: Theory, training, and measurement implications in psychology. *American Psychologist, 68,* 455–466.

Newman, D. (2011). *Identities & inequalities: Exploring the intersections of race, class, gender, and sexuality.* New York, NY: McGraw-Hill.

Pascoe, C. J. (2007). *Dude, you're a fag: Masculinity and sexuality in high school.* Berkley, CA: University of California Press.

Pettigrew, T. F. (2004). Justice deferred: A half century after Brown v. Board of Education. *American Psychologist, 59,* 521–529. Retrieved from http://dx.doi.org/10.1037/0003-066X.59.6.521

Planas, R. (2013, July 15). Arizona objects to Tucson's 'Culturally relevant courses' proposal. *Huffington Post.* Retrieved from http://www.huffingtonpost.com/2013/07/15/arizona-culturally-relevant-courses_n_3599880.html

Roediger, D. R. (2007). *The wages of whiteness: Race and the making of the American working class* (2nd ed.). New York, NY: Verso.

Russell, S. T., Ryan, C., Toomey, R. B., Diaz, R. M., & Sanchez, J. (2011). Lesbian, gay, bisexual and transgender adolescent school victimization: Implications for young adult health and adjustment. *Journal of School Health, 81,* 223–230.

Sanders-Phillips, K. (2009). Racial discrimination: A continuum of violence exposure for children of color. *Clinical Child Family Psychology Review, 12,* 174–195.

Sauntson, H. (2013). Sexual diversity and illocutionary silencing in the English National curriculum. *Sex Education: Sexuality, Society and Learning, 13,* 395–408.

Sellers, R. M., Copeland-Linder, N., Martin, P. P., & Lewis, R. L. (2006). Racial identity matters: The relationship between racial discrimination and psychological functioning in African American adolescents. *Journal of Research on Adolescence, 16,* 187–216. doi: 10.1111/j.1532-7795.2006.00128.x

Smith, E. (2012). *Key issues in education and social justice.* Thousand Oaks, CA: SAGE.

Smith, E. B., & Kuntz, P. (2013, April 30). CEO pay 1,795-to-1 multiple of wages skirts U.S. law. *Bloomberg.* Retrieved from http://www.bloomberg.com/news/2013-04-30/ceo-pay-1-795-to-1-multiple-of-workers-skirts-law-as-sec-delays.html

SPSSI. (n.d.). *Mission statement.* Retrieved from http://www.spssi.org/

Strauss, S. (2012). *Sexual harassment and bullying: A guide to keeping kids safe and holding schools accountable.* Plymouth, UK: Rowman & Littlefield Publishers.

Sue, D. W., Capodilupo, C. M., Torino, G. C., Bucceri, J. M., Holder, A. M. B., Nadal, K. L., & Esquilin, M. (2007). Racial microaggressions in everyday life: Implications for clinical practice. *American Psychologist, 62,* 271–286.

Swearer, S. M., Turner, R. K., Givens, J. E., & Pollack, W. S. (2008). "You're so gay!": Do different forms of bullying matter for adolescent males? *School Psychology Review, 37,* 160–173.

Taylor, M. (2006, February 28). It's official: Class matters. *The Guardian.* Retrieved from http://www.theguardian.com/education/2006/feb/28/schools.education

Toporek, R. L., Gerstein, L., Foud, N., Roysircar, G., & Israel, T. (Eds.). (2006). *Handbook for social justice in counseling psychology.* Thousand Oaks, CA: Sage Publications.

Tummala-Narra, P., & Claudius, M. (2013). Perceived discrimination and depressive symptoms among immigrant-origin adolescents. *Cultural Diversity and Ethnic Minority Psychology, 19,* 257–269. doi: 10.1037/a0032960

Vera, E. M., Buhin, L., & Isacco, A. (2009). The role of prevention in psychology's social justice agenda. In M. E. Kenny, A. M. Horne, P. Orpinas, & L. E. Reese (Eds.), *Realizing social justice: The challenge of preventive interventions* (pp. 79–96). Washington, DC: American Psychological Association.

Weber, K. (2010). *Waiting for superman: How we can save America's failing public schools.* New York, NY: Public Affairs.

Williams, M. T. (2011, December 27). Colorblind ideology is a form of racism: A colorblind approach allows us to deny uncomfortable cultural differences. *Psychology Today.* Retrieved from https://www.psychologytoday.com/blog/culturally-speaking/201112/colorblind-ideology-is-form-racism

Wolff, E. N. (2010). *Recent trends in household wealth in the United States: Rising debt and the middle-class squeeze—An update to 2007* (Levy Economics Institute Working Paper No. 589). Annandale-on-Hudson, NY: Levy Economics Institute of Bard College.

Wong, C. A., Eccles, J. S., & Sameroff, A. (2003). The influence of ethnic discrimination and ethnic identification on African American adolescents' school and socioemotional adjustment. *Journal of Personality, 71,* 1197–1232. doi: 10.1111/1467-6494.7106012

Woo, E. (2005, May 3). Kenneth Clark, 90: His studies influenced ban on segregation. *Los Angeles Times.* Retrieved from http://articles.latimes.com/2005/may/03/local/me-clark3

3 Understanding Identity-Based Bullying Through a Social Constructivist Framework

In addition to understanding identity-based bullying as a social justice issue that impacts everyone within a system (whether it is a school system or society as a whole), I explore this phenomenon using a social constructivist framework. I utilize this approach to provide a deeper understanding of identity-based bullying and how it affects children's lives. First, I explain how I use the social constructivist framework to expand upon the social-ecological model, which has been commonly utilized in anti-bullying work. I then describe how this approach centers children as active agents in their own lives, engaging in meaning making, interpreting and reinterpreting their experiences, and contributing to social norms. I examine how identity-based bullying influences the development of discrimination among children and how it impacts children's identity formation. Finally, I recognize the many ways children are engaged in social change work and encourage educators, scholars, and parents to consider the role children can play in eradicating identity-based bullying.

SOCIAL-ECOLOGICAL MODEL

Most scholars who conduct research on bullying and anti-bullying programs utilize a social-ecological framework to explain how and why bullying occurs (e.g., Espelage & Swearer, 2004; Olweus, 1993; Swearer & Doll, 2001). This framework situates the individual (be they a bully or a victim) within a series of systems that influence their behavior. The social-ecological model centers the experience of the individual (as the bullseye) with the systems surrounding the individual in increasing levels (family, school, community, etc.). The framework stems from Brofenbrenner's (1979) ecological systems theory examining the interconnectedness of four systems: the microsystem, mesosystem, exosystem, and macrosystem. Within anti-bullying work, the model is often applied to examine how factors at different levels (individual, family, school, community, culture) can impact bullying. For example, research at the microsystem level may include studies examining how school climate impacts bullying. Climates in which students internalize prosocial norms

40 *Social Constructivist Framework*

and values of the school have reduced levels of bullying (Ma, 2001), while school climates that condone bullying, are high in conflict, and disorganized have higher levels of bullying behaviors (Espelage & Swearer, 2004).

While the social-ecological framework recognizes that students play an active role in their environments, the model is often used to emphasize how different systems affect children, including arguments for the need to both assess and change multiple areas (i.e., what is the school culture around bullying, what is happening within the family, etc.). Interestingly, although arrows are rarely shown, explanations of the model often focus on one direction of influence, exploring how the outer levels affect the child at the center (left arrow). This approach neglects to recognize that the influence is bidirectional—a child is being impacted while simultaneously impacting the surrounding systems (right arrow).

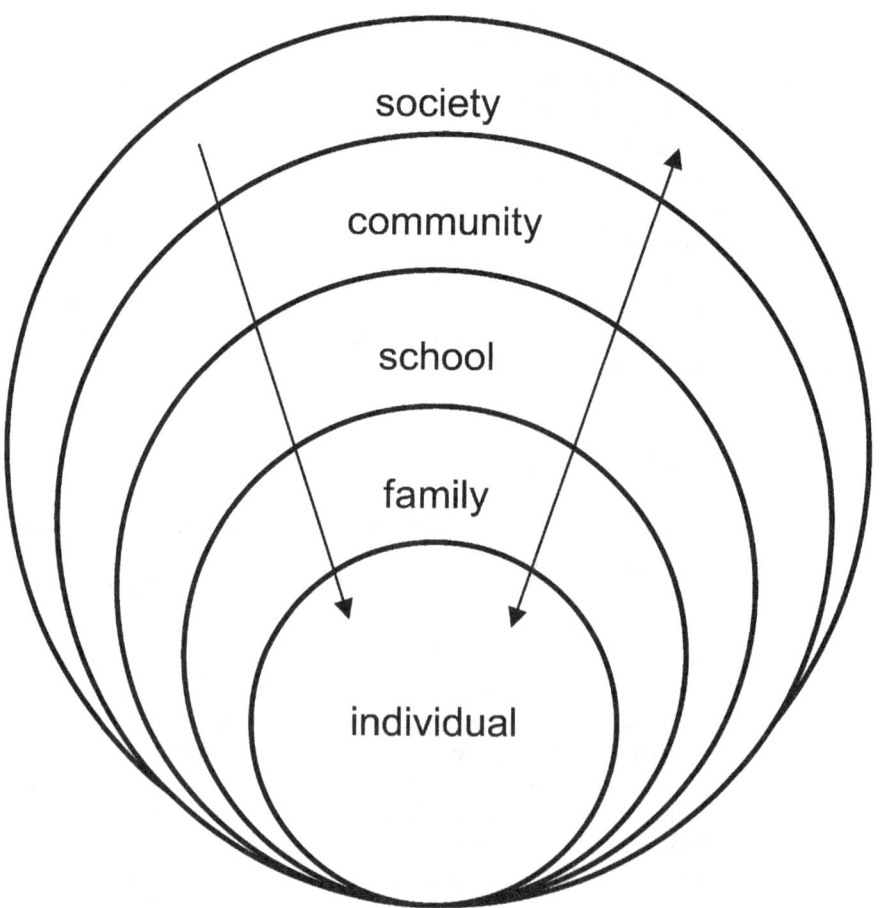

Figure 3.1 Social-Ecological Model

SOCIAL CONSTRUCTIVIST APPROACH

Constructivist theories within psychology are those that emphasize the ways humans create meaning in their world. Raskin (2002) argues that there are several varieties of constructivist theories; and although there is philosophical overlap among them, there is sometimes confusion about the distinctions. This is made even more complex by terminology. Some theorists (such as Kenneth Gergen, 1985) prefer the term *social constructionism* to *social constructivism* but many use the terms interchangeably. The differences between the two appear to be whether the focus is on the individual processes (social constructivism) or the group product of these processes (social constructionism) (Andrews, 2012; Young & Collin, 2004). No one theorist is credited with developing social constructivism, but various scholars have contributed to the literature about the approach. Many consider Lev Vygotsky's (1978) theories regarding childhood development to be some of the earliest social constructivist approaches within psychology. Vygotsky emphasized the role of social interactions in learning and asserted that cultural and societal values influence how children learn.

While the individual theories have distinctions among them, as a group, constructivist theories are distinguished from other philosophical approaches by their emphasis on the creation (rather than discovery) of reality (Sexton, 1997). Constructivist approaches assert that there is no one reality or *Truth* that can be discovered. Instead, human beings make meaning within their circumstances, and these meanings always reflect a perspective or worldview. Constructivist thinking exists in contrast to modernism, which emphasizes logic and the search for truth. From such a modernist approach, scientists are expected to be neutral and without bias in order to uncover information (Sexton, 1997). Rather than focusing on the discovery of "unbiased" information, constructivist approaches emphasize increased knowledge about the processes through which humans make meaning and greater recognition of factors that influence one's perceptions and experiences of the world. In addition to identifying the constructed nature of reality, social constructivist perspectives focus on "the interdependence of social and individual processes in the co-construction of knowledge" (Palincsar, 1998).

Utilizing a social constructivist perspective, I assert that it is important to recognize the influence of multiple levels of interactions (including the range from micro to macro), *and* it is necessary to view children as active participants being influenced by and having an influence upon these environments. In this way, the social constructivist approach exists not in contrast to the social-ecological model, but rather expands upon this conceptualization of bullying by examining the complexities that result from the active role children play in creating their own reality. This approach provides a framework for exploring how children make meaning within their own social systems (including schools). Social constructivism centers the child as an active agent in this meaning-making process. I utilize a social constructivist perspective in this book to explore how identity-based bullying is a mechanism that reflects and reinforces discrimination and to examine how identity-based bullying impacts the identity development of children. Finally, I examine the processes by which children can (and are) engaged in change making—recognizing children as agents to promote social justice.

CHILDREN ARE ACTIVE AGENTS

The primary way that the social constructivist perspective expands upon the social-ecological approach is the emphasis on children actively engaging in constructing meaning in their world. The social constructivist perspective includes the recognition that children are agents in the processes of developing prejudicial attitudes and in their own identity-development process. Rather than passively absorbing discrimination, children learn stereotypes and reinforce and teach them during their interactions with others. It is important to note that this active process does not imply that children are always intentionally discriminating against others, nor are they always aware of the impact of their actions. However, children are active participants in systems that more often than not reinforce and reward such behavior. As a result, children may make decisions (with varying degrees of self-awareness) about how to best thrive in such a system and how to avoid undesirable outcomes (such as becoming a target of identity-based bullying).

Just as the influence of the environment on the child can serve to either increase or decrease identity-based bullying, so too can the influence of the child on the environment be positive or negative. Children who engage in identity-based bullying may increase the likelihood that others (including their targets and bystanders) will engage in similar or reciprocal behaviors. In contrast, children who resist stereotypes and challenge others who perpetrate identity-based bullying may have positive impacts on their environments. For example, students who become involved in gay-straight alliances in schools may shift the culture of the school so it becomes a safer space for LGBT students, while also motivating change among the other students, teachers, and staff within those schools. Those individual players may then go on to impact other environments by challenging homophobic comments made by family members, supporting LGBT rights through voting practices, etc.

Labeling Roles—Not Children

From a social constructivist perspective, children cannot be simply categorized as bullies, targets, or bystanders. Rather, an individual child may enact any one of these roles depending upon the particular circumstances and context. Throughout the book, I at times refer to a target (or victim), bystander, or bully but use these words to signify the role a child is engaged in during a particular incidence rather than to label them permanently with one of these three identities. While some children tend to find themselves most often in one of these roles, others will occupy all of these roles at different points. In fact, Nansel et al. (2001) found that about 6% of children in their study reported frequently being a target and frequently being a bully.

Rather than identifying a particular child as a *bully*, the social constructivist approach calls on us to explore the circumstances under which a child engages in bullying. This change in perspective can shift the way teachers, administrators, and parents seek to treat and prevent identity-based bullying. Instead of focusing primarily on identifying and changing "difficult" individuals, this approach emphasizes changing the social and structural conditions that lead to identity-based bullying. This also moves away from an approach that pathologizes the individuals engaging in the behavior to one that challenges the patriarchal structures that reinforce it (Brown, Chesney-Lind, & Stein, 2007). I am particularly interested in highlighting the social and environmental factors that impact identity-based bullying, but it is important to note that a body of research has attempted to understand why individual children are more or less likely to act as bullies. While that is not the focus of this book, I encourage readers to review literature about these factors (such as Orpinas & Horne, 2006).

Individual children may engage in identity-based bullying in some contexts but not in others. For example, Pascoe's (2007) observations of young men in one high school illustrate the ways that young men may attempt to appear stereotypically masculine by engaging in derogatory "locker room talk" and presenting themselves as being sexually experienced. While Pascoe witnessed lots of sexual harassment in the hallways and boys in groups talking about young women in sexually objectifying and degrading ways, she experienced a different perspective when meeting with the young men individually. When they were removed from their peer groups (groups who frequently policed masculinity through bullying), many of these young men talked about their relationships with girls in nonobjectifying ways. They were respectful and kind and admitted to their own insecurities about romantic and sexual relationships. These differences in language and behavior suggest that boys' engagement in sexual harassment and identity-based bullying may be context dependent. Working with boys and young men to change the parameters of these contexts may be more effective at deterring identity-based bullying than labeling boys (individually or as a group) as bullies or harassers.

Some bullying scholars advocate that anti-bullying programs should encourage children to recognize how they might be contributing to their vulnerability as a victim (Fried & Soslan, 2011). I caution educators against adopting such an approach, as it may function to maintain power differentials and signal to students that they are expected to be responsible for protecting themselves from mistreatment from others. In fact, a social justice perspective on this issue asserts that educators should support those who are being oppressed and work to dismantle the system of oppression, not reinforce it with our own actions. It is possible for adults to have frank conversations with children being targeted with identity-based bullying without victim blaming or telling children that they should change in order to avoid being bullied. In fact, many children probably already consider (or already attempt) altering their behaviors in the hopes of minimizing their vulnerability. Instead, adult educators can open discussions about a child's identity in a way that affirms that the child has a right to his or her own identity (to dress and act authentically) and explore with the child how he or she would like to address the bullying, keeping at the forefront the goal of empowering the target rather than further victimizing the child.

IDENTITY-BASED BULLYING AND DEVELOPMENT OF PREJUDICE AND DISCRIMINATION

The development of discriminatory beliefs and attitudes toward others (which can lead to engaging in identity-based bullying) happens over time and through a variety of mechanisms. Most social scientists believe that children are not born with stereotypes but learn them in various ways throughout their lives (Aboud, 2005; Allport, 1958; Derman-Sparks & Phillips, 1997; Dovidio & Gaertner, 1986). During late childhood into early adolescence, children develop social skills and cognitive skills that impact their peer interactions and increase the likelihood of engaging in identity-based bullying (Nesdale, 2004). Research and opinion varies as to what factors have the most influence over children's development of prejudicial beliefs and the adoption of discriminatory behaviors, but most experts include the possible influence of parents/family of origin, peers, adults outside the home, social systems (especially school systems where children spend a considerable amount of their time), and media. The attitudes that children are exposed to can impact the development of their thoughts and behaviors well into adulthood (Abrams & Killen, 2014).

Identity-based bullying is one form of discrimination, and it is also a method through which children learn prejudicial attitudes and stereotypes. Children who witness others being teased, called derogatory terms, excluded, or mistreated because of some aspect of their identity may internalize the messages being sent during these events. In this way, identity-based bullying serves as a mechanism through which discrimination is both taught and reinforced, often in a cyclical manner that can seem challenging to interrupt.

Children learn both descriptive stereotypes (stereotypes that purport to describe the world as it is) and prescriptive stereotypes (those that describe expectations about how the world should be) (Burgess & Borgida, 1999; Eagly, 1987) from identity-based bullying. Children can come to believe the stereotypes embedded in these interactions, whether they are based on one's religion, ethnicity, gender, social class, or sexual orientation. Descriptive stereotypes may be particularly likely to be internalized if the observer has little direct experience with individuals within the target group. For example, White children living in communities where they have little to no interaction with children of color may hold more stereotypical attitudes about non-White racial groups. In fact, the theory of intergroup contact suggests that when individuals interact with others who are from groups different than them, their attitudes about members of that group often become less discriminatory (Pettigrew, 1998). One meta-analysis of over 500 studies found that intergroup contact does usually reduce intergroup prejudice (Pettigrew & Tropp, 2006).

Children may also internalize prescriptive stereotypes learned by witnessing and experiencing identity-based bullying. These types of stereotypes may be held against groups with whom one is familiar. For example, most children have many interactions with boys and girls, yet may still hold prejudicial beliefs regarding gender. Some stereotypes about gender are descriptive, but many are also prescriptive, meaning that they include expectations about how one should or should not behave (e.g., girls *should* be nice, boys *should not* cry) (Prentice & Carranza, 2002). Prescriptive stereotypes often persist despite interactions with individuals from various groups. Contrary to descriptive stereotypes, which may be dispelled by interacting with an individual who does not fit the stereotype, prescriptive stereotypes might be reinforced in situations where one is not conforming to them (Burgess & Borgida, 1999). Rather than dispelling stereotypes as being incorrect assumptions, children may police each other's behaviors according to prescriptive stereotypes. For example, a boy who demonstrates emotions (perhaps by crying) may actually trigger the prescriptive stereotype that boys should not be emotional rather than challenge the belief that boys "naturally" are not.

Children's internalization of stereotypes may change throughout their childhood and is shaped by their own identities and experiences. Baker and Fishbein (1998) found that adolescents' prejudice toward gays and lesbians increased from grades seven to nine. Anti-LGBT attitudes among girls then decreased from grades nine to eleven but increased for boys during this same time. Such gender differences in adopting homophobic attitudes are likely influenced by boys' own experiences of socialization. During adolescence, most boys experience increased pressure to conform to hegemonic masculinity, which often includes distancing themselves from anything that could be perceived as gay (Kimmel, 2009; Klein, 2006; Pollack, 1998). Baker and Fishbein (1998) also found that girls held more prejudicial attitudes against lesbians, while boys held more prejudicial attitudes against gays, further suggesting that students' stereotypical views are in some ways related to their own identity. Heterosexual students may be less understanding toward an individual of their same sex who is different from them.

IDENTITY-BASED BULLYING AND IDENTITY FORMATION

The social constructivist perspective provides a framework to examine one of the ways in which identity-based bullying affects children, namely by influencing their identity-development process. Constructivist approaches (like personal construct theory) argue that the self is constructed rather than discovered (Raskin, 2002). One way that children create their identities is through their interactions with others. Pahl and Way (2006) found that adolescents who experienced racial slurs and harassment were more likely to question what it meant to belong to their ethnic group. Children in negatively stereotyped groups may also begin to think about their group memberships earlier than do children in privileged groups (Brown, Alabi, Huynh, & Masten, 2011). I have witnessed this phenomenon in my own work with children. White children are often less likely to identify their own ethnicity than are children of color. Even for children of color, their experiences of being surrounded by other children of color versus mostly White children can impact their identity development. Huang and Stormshak (2011) conducted a longitudinal study of identity development to understand the process by which children of color think about their ethnicity throughout adolescence. Their findings suggested that children who attend homogenous schools differ in their identity development when compared to children from ethnically diverse schools.

Children's identity emerges as a result of a dynamic negotiation process in which children react and respond to experiences of prejudice, including identity-based bullying (for more on this identity-development process as it relates to gender, see Brinkman, Rabenstein, Rosén, & Zimmerman, 2014). Identity-based bullying may impact children's construction of their identity in a myriad of ways. Children who are directly targeted may feel shame about an aspect of their identity, may internalize stereotypes about a group to which they belong, or may hide or deny an aspect of their identity.

INTERNALIZATION OF STEREOTYPES

One way that children's identity-development process may be negatively impacted by identity-based bullying is through the internalization of stereotypes about groups to which they belong. Scholars have argued that internalized racial oppression among Black Americans results from accepting White culture's oppressive and racist beliefs toward Black people (Bailey, Chung, Williams, Singh, & Terrell, 2011). LGB young adults who experienced bullying as adolescents have reported that they learned to internalize homophobia as a response to witnessing and experiencing identity-based bullying in schools (Mishna et al., 2009). Children who grow up hearing the terms *fag* or *gay* being used as slurs may internalize negative beliefs about homosexuality, possibly before they are even aware of their own sexual orientation. Girls who reach puberty earlier than their peers are often targeted with sexual harassment and gender-based bullying (Duncan, 1999). These girls may be told that they are targets of inappropriate behavior because of their physical maturation and may internalize such victim-blaming messages. Such experiences may shape the way a girl thinks about herself as a sexual person. Girls may also internalize these messages in the form of self-objectification—a state in which a person views herself/himself as an object (Fredrickson & Roberts, 1997; Moradi & Huang, 2008; Slater & Tiggemann, 2002).

Children may also internalize the beliefs underlying identity-based bullying as a result of the lack of intervention by adults. For example, girls who experience sexual harassment and witness teachers ignoring or minimizing the behavior may learn to expect others will treat them like sex objects. In one British school, girls discussed their experiences of gender-based bullying (particularly being called derogatory names) in a way that demonstrated their dislike of the behavior but also their perception of their inability to change it. "Their view was that it existed in their world like litter; ubiquitous, unpleasant and unnecessary, but usually not personal or hurtful and in any case, too well established for them to do anything about it" (Duncan, 1999, p. 40). Not surprisingly, most of these girls did not report their experiences to school personnel or parents; they did not believe that it would be effective to do so. Some thought the school would not adequately handle the situation, some worried that they would actually be blamed for the behavior.

Internalizing negative beliefs about an aspect of one's identity can have damaging consequences for a child. Children who have internalized oppression may engage in self-destructive behaviors, believe in a biased representation of history, and attempt to change their physical appearance to look more like the majority culture (Bailey et al., 2011). In contrast, adolescents who develop a secure sense of self—including a feeling of belonging to one's group and a sense of pride and positive feelings about their ethnic group— have higher self-esteem and overall mental health (Brook, Balka, Brook, Win & Gursen, 1998; Greig, 2003; Miller & MacIntosh, 1999). Individuals who experience identity-based bullying may have a more challenging time developing a positive sense of their identity if they internalize the negative messages that others convey about their group.

Avoiding Behaviors or Experiences

Identity-based bullying may also change the way in which a child's identity forms through his or her avoidance of particular behaviors or experiences. For example, numerous theorists have argued that boys are encouraged to embrace traditionally masculine traits and behaviors (e.g., being physically strong, engaging in risk-taking behaviors) and to reject feminine ones (Good & Sherrod, 2001; Kimmel, 2009, Pollack, 1999). In fact, the theory of *precarious manhood* asserts that manhood is an elusive and tenuous state of being and it is possible for one to lose his manhood status if he does not behave in ascribed ways (Vandello & Bosson, 2013; Vandello, Bosson, Cohen, Burnaford, & Weaver, 2008). Kimmel (2009) argues that there is a *guycode* among adolescent and college age men in which they are expected to both engage in gender performance and critique each other's presentations of masculinity. Among children, identity-based bullying can be one way to pressure others to conform to gender stereotypes. In an attempt to avoid being bullied, individuals may choose to hide aspects of themselves that do not conform to traditional gender norms. In my own work with children, I have heard many fifth and sixth grade boys talk about ways that they protected themselves by hiding something about their identity. One boy described how much he liked his sister's Barbie computer game, but he would only play it with her and never when his male friends were around.

Identity-based bullying likely impacts the development of other aspects of identity in a similar way. For example, Liu, Soleck, Hopps, Dunston, and Pickett (2004) identify insulation as one of the common responses to interpersonal classism. In response to class-based bullying, children might learn to insulate themselves and attempt to only spend time with others of a similar social class to protect themselves and stay congruent to their own identity. In doing so, they might limit their exposure to experiences that they deem to be not appropriate for members of their social class and lose opportunities to expand their interests and abilities.

A Dynamic and Complex Process

The impact that identity-based bullying has on children's identity development is not static but rather involves a dynamic process. Children help construct identity categories—they create meaning by defining, resisting, and reinforcing messages about identity. For example, children and adolescents do not simply conform to gender role expectations as defined by adults, but they are actively challenging them, commenting on them, and engaging in their own construction of gender (and the policing of others' performance of gender) (Eder, Evans, & Stephen, 1995). Children's experiences of identity-based bullying may also influence the extent to which they focus on or highlight aspects of their identity in given situations. Deaux and Major (1987) argue that gender-related behaviors are impacted by the expectations of others within a situation as well as contextual cues. Children who are exposed to ideas suggesting that their gender or ethnicity are associated with negative attributes or outcomes (such as being excluded) place less importance on that aspect of their identity in those situations (Turner & Brown, 2007).

While the link between identity-based bullying and identity performance seems clear, the impact on a child's internal experience of their identity is harder to pinpoint. West and Zimmerman (1987) argue that in many ways gender is a performance—it is something one *does* rather than something one *is*. As a result, children may present an outward performance of their gender that is both congruent and incongruent with their internal selves. A boy may deny his love of ballet but emphasize his interest in football. However, identity-based bullying may influence the development of children's internal selves if children limit their exposure to certain people or activities. In that way, a boy may never develop a love of ballet because he denied himself opportunities to try it in order to avoid being teased about participating in a "feminine" activity. Consider also a girl who rarely practices being assertive because doing so early on in life resulted in her being called *bossy* or *bitchy*. While assertiveness may be a part of the *performance* of gender, at what point does the lack of engaging in the behavior change the child's ability/interest to do so? It is challenging to pinpoint where the line is drawn between gender performance and gender identity. Nevertheless, identity-based bullying may shape children's gender identity, not just their gender performance, and limit the potential of who they might otherwise become.

CHILDREN CREATING SOCIAL CHANGE

Viewing children as being actively involved in the creation of their own reality may encourage educators to consider the possibility that children can play an active role in identity-based bullying prevention and intervention efforts. Unfortunately, the perspectives of children have often been neglected in research about children. Many adults appear to assume that children will be unable to speak articulately about their own needs, wants, and feelings and must have adults speak for them. As Abrams and Killen (2014) note, because children lack social, political, and economic power, they are often excluded from conversations about policy making—even when those policies directly impact them. Children who are marginalized because of some aspect of their identity are even less likely to have a voice, as adults who share their identity may also be excluded from conversations. While adults are certainly able to provide important information about what occurs in schools, studies that give children opportunities to speak for themselves shed important light on their perspectives about equity in schools.

Children and adolescents are sometimes excluded from conversations about identity because of adult assumptions regarding their ability to handle some topics. In her work studying masculinity in high schools, Pascoe (2007) writes about the resistance she experienced from school administrators who were concerned that she may discuss sexuality with the students. The school administrators encouraged her to avoid any discussions of sex. "They reflected the twin assumptions that American teens are too innocent to know about sexuality and too sexual to be trusted with information" (p. 29). This attitude is reflected in many school officials' approaches to addressing diversity issues in schools. When teachers and administrators assume that students are not capable of understanding these issues or dynamics, they often dismiss the insights that children can and do possess. Attempts to recognize and prevent identity-based bullying will be more successful when students are actively included in the work.

Viewing children as active agents in creating reality calls for a shift in thinking about the role of education and educators. A co-intentional model of education (Freire, 1970) emphasizes the role of teachers and students as both subjects in unveiling, creating, and recreating knowledge. This approach engages all parties and creates commitment to the educational pursuit that is different from an approach in which students are expected to be passive learners. When given the opportunity to do so, children can and do clearly articulate their dreams of what schooling should be. In their study of racist bullying within schools, Richardson and Miles (2008) gathered the voices of British children through focus groups, interviews, and individual workshops. The children spoke about their experiences of racism within schools, as well as their hopes for a better and more just school environment. In 2001, the *Guardian* newspaper in the United Kingdom held an essay competition in which they encouraged students to write on the subject "the school I'd like" (Burke & Grosvenor, 2003). The results of the 2001 competition were compiled into a Children's Manifesto, describing the children's descriptions of their dream school. The striking thing about this competition was that a number of children spoke about their desire for school to reflect social justice principles, for all children to be treated well and with fairness. A follow-up competition was held in 2011 during which a Year 7 student wrote, "The school I'd like would be where everyone's equal, and everybody's respected and their voices are heard." (Smith, 2012, p. 83).

Many students are already proactively engaged in efforts to support social change and decrease identity-based bullying. For example, in one school, a group of students fought hard to start a gay-straight alliance and won, despite reluctance from the administrators (Pascoe, 2007). Batsleer (2012) describes how lesbian and gay youth in Britain banded together to create spaces that promote social justice. By channeling their negative experiences into energy to support change, these youth are improving the culture for their peers and other young adults. Engaging in activism and educating others can also be empowering for the individual doing it. Pendragon (2010) described how some sexual minority female youth utilized activism as a method of coping with their own negative experiences. They were able to reach out to others and find a community of support, but they also felt that their resistance to others' discrimination helped protect them from the potential harm to their well-being.

CONCLUSION

The social constructivist approach asserts that children are not born to engage in prejudice but rather are taught, reinforced, and rewarded for patterns of thinking and acting that value some individuals' experiences over others. This approach means not labeling children as either victims or perpetrators of bullying but rather expands our thinking about bullying to encompass the complexities involved. It includes recognizing how identity-based bullying can impact children's identity development, often in restrictive or harmful ways. Social constructivist approaches also allow for one to see the potential for change to happen, as they assert that meaning is constructed and thus can be challenged and reconstructed. By acknowledging children as active agents in their own lived experiences, scholars, teachers, administrators, and parents can take an important step toward eradicating identity-based bullying. If adults give them the opportunity to do so, many children and adolescents will be at the forefront of a movement for change.

REFERENCES

Aboud, F. (2005). The development of prejudice in childhood and adolescence. In J. F. Dovidio, P. Glick, & L. Rudman (Eds.), *On the nature of prejudice: Fifty years after Allport* (pp. 310–326). Malden, MA: Blackwell Publishing.

Abrams, D., & Killen, M. (2014). Social exclusion of children: Developmental origins of prejudice. *Journal of Social Issues, 70,* 1–11. doi: 10.1111/josi.12043

Allport, G. (1958). *The nature of prejudice.* Reading, MA: Addison, Wesley.

Andrews, T. (2012). What is social constructionism? *Grounded Theory Review, 11,* 39–46.

Bailey, T. K. M., Chung, Y. B., Williams, W. S., Singh, A. A., & Terrell, H. (2011). Development and validation of the internalized racial oppression scale for Black individuals. *Journal of Counseling Psychology, 58,* 481–493. Retrieved from http://dx.doi.org/10.1037/a0023585

Baker, J. G., & Fishbein, H. D. (1998). The development of prejudice towards gays and lesbians by adolescents. *Journal of Homosexuality, 36,* 89–100. doi: 10.1300/J082v36n01_06

Batsleer, J. (2012). Dangerous spaces, dangerous memories, dangerous emotions: Informal education and heteronormativity—A Manchester UK youth work vignette. *Discourse: Studies in the Cultural Politics of Education, 33,* 345–360. doi: 10.1080/01596306.2012.681896

Brinkman, B. G., Rabenstein, K., Rosén, L., & Zimmerman, T. (2014). Children's gender identity development: A dynamic negotiation between conformity and authenticity. *Youth and Society, 46,* 835–852.

Brofenbrenner, U. (1979). *The ecology of human development: Experiments by nature and design.* Cambridge, MA: Harvard University Press.

Brook, J. S., Balka, E. B., Brook, D. W., Win, P. T., & Gursen, M. D. (1998). Drug use among African Americans: Ethnic identity as a protective factor. *Psychological Reports, 83,* 1427–1446. doi: 10.2466/pr0.1998.83.3f.1427

Brown, C. S., Alabi, B. O., Huynh, V. W., & Masten, C. L. (2011). Ethnicity and gender in late childhood and early adolescence: Group identity and awareness of bias. *Developmental Psychology, 47,* 463–471.

Brown, L. M., Chesney-Lind, M., & Stein, N. (2007). Patriarchy matters: Toward a gendered theory of teen violence and victimization. *Violence Against Women, 13,* 1249–1273. doi: 10.1177/1077801207310430

Burgess, D., & Borgida, E. (1999). Who women are, who women should be: Descriptive and prescriptive gender stereotyping in sex discrimination. *Psychology, public policy, and Law, 5,* 665–692. Retrieved from http://dx.doi.org/10.1037/1076-8971.5.3.665

Burke, C., & Grosvenor, I. (2003). *The school I'd like: Children and young people's reflections on education for the 21st Century*. London, UK: RoutledgeFalmer.
Deaux, K., & Major, B. (1987). Putting gender into context: An interactive model of gender-related behavior. *Psychological Review, 94*, 369–389.
Derman-Sparks, L., & Phillips, C. B. (1997). *Teaching/learning anti-racism: A developmental approach*. New York, NY: Teachers College Press.
Dovidio, J. F., & Gaertner, S. L. (1986). *Prejudice, discrimination, and racism*. Orlando, FL: Academic Press.
Duncan, N. (1999). *Sexual bullying: Gender conflict and pupil culture in secondary schools*. London, England: Routledge.
Eagly, A. H. (1987). *Sex differences in social behavior: A social-role interpretation*. Hillsdale, NJ: Erlbaum.
Eder, D., Evans, C. C., & Stephen, P. (1995). *School talk: Gender and adolescent culture*. New Brunswick, NJ: Rutgers University Press.
Espelage, D. L., & Swearer, S. M. (2004). *Bullying in American schools: A social-ecological perspective on prevention and intervention*. Mahwah, NJ: Lawrence Erlbaum Associates.
Fredrickson, B. L., & Roberts, T. (1997). Objectification theory. *Psychology of Women Quarterly, 21*, 173–206. doi: 10.1111/j.1471-6402.1997.tb00108.x
Freire, P. (1970). *Pedagogy of the oppressed*. New York, NY: The Continuum International Publishing Group.
Fried, S., & Soslan, B. (2011). *Banishing bullying behavior: Transforming the culture of peer abuse* (2nd ed.). Lanham, MD: Rowman & Littlefield Education.
Gergen, K. J. (1985). The social constructionist movement in modern psychology. *American Psychologist, 40*, 266–275.
Good, G. G., & Sherrod, N. B. (2001). The psychology of men and masculinity: Research status and future directions. In R. K. Unger (Ed.), *Handbook of the psychology of women and gender* (pp. 201–214). New York, NY: Wiley.
Greig, R. (2003). Ethnic Identity development: Implications for mental health in African-American and Hispanic adolescents. *Issues in Mental Health Nursing, 24*, 317–331.
Huang, C. Y., & Stormshak, E. A. (2011). A longitudinal examination of early adolescence ethnic identity trajectories. *Cultural Diversity and Ethnic Minority Psychology, 17*, 261–270. doi: 10.1037/a0023882
Kimmel, M. (2009). *Guyland: The perilous world where boys become men*. New York, NY: Harper Collins Publishers.
Klein, J. (2006). Cultural capital and high school bullies: How social inequality impacts school violence. *Men and Masculinities, 9*, 53–75. doi: 10.1177/1097184X04271387
Liu, W. M., Soleck, G., Hopps, J., Dunston, K., & Pickett, T. (2004). A new framework to understand social class in counseling: The social class worldview and modern classism theory. *Journal of Multicultural Counseling and Development, 32*, 95–122. doi: 10.1002/j.2161-1912.2004.tb00364.x
Ma, X. (2001). Bullying and being bullied: To what extent are bullies also victims? *American Educational Research Journal, 38*, 351–570.
Miller, D. B., & MacIntosh, R. (1999). Promoting resilience in urban African American adolescents: Racial socialization and identity as protective factors. *Social Work Research, 23*, 159–169. doi: 10.1093/swr/23.3.159
Mishna, F., Newman, P. A., Daley, A., & Solomon, S. (2009). Bullying of lesbian and gay youth: A qualitative investigation. *The British Journal of Social Work, 39*, 1598–1614.
Moradi, B., & Huang, Y. P. (2008). Objectification theory and psychology of women: A decade of advances and future directions. *Psychology of Women Quarterly, 32*, 377–398. doi: 10.1111/j.1471-6402.2008.00452.x

Nansel, T., Overpeck, M., Pilla, R., Ruan, W., Simons-Morton, B., & Scheidt, P. (2001). Bullying behaviors among U.S. youth: Prevalence and association with psychosocial adjustment. *JAMA, 285*, 2094–2100.

Nesdale, D. (2004). Social identity processes and children's ethnic prejudice. In M. Bennett & F. Sani (Eds.), *The development of the social self* (pp. 219–245). New York, NY: Psychology Press.

Olweus, D. (1993). *Bullying at school: What we know and what we can do.* Oxford, UK: Blackwell.

Orpinas, P., & Horne, A. M. (2006). *Bullying Prevention: Creating a positive school climate and developing social competencies.* Washington, DC: American Psychological Association.

Pahl, K., & Way, N. (2006). Longitudinal trajectories of ethnic identity among urban Black and Latino adolescents. *Child Development, 77*, 1403–1415. doi: 10.1111/j.1467-8624.2006.00943.x

Palincsar, A. S. (1998). Social constructivist perspectives on teaching and learning. *Annual Review of Psychology, 49*, 345–375.

Pascoe, C.J. (2007). *Dude, you're a fag: Masculinity and sexuality in high school.* Berkley, CA: University of California Press.

Pendragon, D.K. (2010). Coping behaviors among sexual minority female youth. *Journal of Lesbian Studies, 14*, 5–15.

Pettigrew, T. F. (1998). Intergroup contact theory. *Annual Review of Psychology, 49*, 65–85.

Pettigrew, T. F., & Tropp, L. R. (2006). A meta-analytic test of intergroup contact theory. *Journal of Personality and Social Psychology, 90*, 751–783. Retrieved from http://dx.doi.org/10.1037/0022-3514.90.5.751

Pollack, W. (1998). *Real boys: Rescuing our sons from the myths of boyhood.* Henry Hold and Company, NY: New York.

Pollack, W. (1999). The sacrifice of Isaac: Toward a new psychology of boys and men. *The Society for the Psychological Study of Men and Masculinity, 4*, 7–14.

Prentice, D. A., & Carranza, E. (2002). What women and men should be, shouldn't be, are allowed to be, and don't have to be: The contents of prescriptive gender stereotypes. *Psychology of Women Quarterly, 26*, 269–281. doi: 10.1111/1471-6402.t01-1-00066

Raskin, J. D. (2002). Constructivism in psychology: Personal construct psychology, radical constructivism, and social constructionism. *American Communication Journal, 5*, 1–24.

Richardson, R., & Miles, B. (2008). *Racist incidents and bullying in schools.* Staffordshire, UK: Trentham Books Limited.

Sexton, T.L. (1997). Constructivist thinking within the history of ideas: The challenge of a new paradigm. In T.L. Sexton & B.L. Griffin (Eds.), *Constructivist thinking in counseling practice, research, and training* (pp. 3–18). New York, NY: Teachers College Press.

Slater, A., & Tiggemann, M. (2002). A test of objectification theory in adolescent girls. *Sex Roles, 46*, 343–349. doi: 10.1023/A:1020232714705

Smith, E. (2012). *Key issues in education and social justice.* Thousand Oaks, CA: SAGE.

Swearer, S.M., & Doll, B. (2001). Bullying in schools: An ecological framework. *Journal of Emotional Abuse, 2*, 7–23.

Turner, K.L., & Brown, C.S. (2007). The centrality of gender and ethnic identities across individuals and contexts. *Social Development, 16*, 700–719. doi: 10.1111/j.1467-9507.2007.00403.x

Vandello, J. A., & Bosson, J. K. (2013). Hard won and easily lost: A review and synthesis of theory and research on precarious manhood. *Psychology of Men and Masculinity, 14*, 101–113. doi: 10.1037/a0029826101

Vandello, J. A., Bosson, J. K., Cohen, D., Burnaford, R. M., & Weaver, J. R. (2008). Precarious manhood. *Journal of Personality and Social Psychology, 95,* 1325–1339. doi: 10.1037/a0012453

Vygotsky, L. S. (1978). *Mind in society.* Cambridge, MA: Harvard University Press.

West, C., & Zimmerman, D. H. (1987). Doing gender. *Gender & Society, 1,* 125–151.

Young, R., & Collin, A. (2004). Introduction: Constructivism and social constructionism in the career field. *Journal of Vocational Behaviour, 64,* 373–388.

4 Cultural Factors Influencing Identity-Based Bullying

Individuals who spend much of their time within a school (including both children and adults) often *feel* like the school is a world of its own; therefore, educators may be tempted to focus predominantly on factors within a given educational setting when developing anti-bullying programs. While it is essential to examine the particular climate of each school (as I discuss in more depth in Chapters 5 and 7), there is much we can learn about the way identity-based bullying manifests in schools (and how to eradicate it) by exploring cultural influences.

In this chapter, I describe how identity-based bullying is both reflected in and influenced by cultural factors. I provide examples of social inequalities and prejudices that can manifest as identity-based bullying within a school. I examine cultural influences through a variety of avenues, including policies and laws regarding social issues and representations of identity within popular media. This chapter is not meant to be a comprehensive list of such occurrences but rather a selection of examples to demonstrate the connection between events occurring within a society and bullying happening within schools. The coverage will include: income inequalities and prejudice against the poor, battles over legal rights for LGBT individuals, and discrimination based on race/ethnicity and religion. In each of these areas, I present information about both the United States and the United Kingdom (recognizing that some factors impact both nations). This selection of topics is not intended to minimize the importance of exploring cultural influences on other types of identity-based bullying, and it is my hope that scholars and educators will expand upon this analysis, using these examples as guides for doing so.

PREJUDICE AGAINST THE POOR

Although some could (and do) argue that children's conflicts regarding wealth simply reflect a tendency to highlight differences within a group, an examination of the broader cultural context within the U.S. and the U.K.

reveals how children's class-based conflict mirror conflicts happening among adults. In both nations, there exist very real divides based on social class and children often are disproportionately impacted. According to the U.S. Census Bureau, the total population poverty rate in 2013 was 14.5%, but the poverty rate for children under 18 was 19.9%. A recent report released within the U.K. (Peachey, Smith, & Sharma, 2013) reported a disturbing trend of increasing utilization of emergency food services and indicated that in 2013 over half a million children lived in families who were unable to consistently provide them with a minimally acceptable diet. In addition to children being directly impacted by poverty, they may experience identity-based bullying based on their social class.

Children are exposed to stereotypes about the poor through their families, the media, and within school. They may internalize these stereotypes and then interact with their peers based on these beliefs and attitudes. This internalized classism can then manifest itself among children through teasing (Liu, Soleck, Hopps, Dunston, & Pickett, 2004), ostracism, and other forms of identity-based bullying. In particular, students who are believed to have less wealth/resources than others may be targeted for identity-based bullying. Children may not know their own family's actual net worth, let alone that of other families, yet they turn to a variety of markers to assess the financial situation of other children. Some of these markers of wealth are concrete, while others indicate the relative position of a child compared to the mean. As Klein (2006) noticed, the brands of clothing that were worn by the wealthier students at one school were the brands worn by the poorer students at another school. The key issue resides not in the actual amount of money that a family has, but the relative position of wealth that student has compared to others in their school. The fact that students find ways to identify the highest and lowest within a group (even if most students are similar in social class) mirrors the social class hierarchy that exists outside of any single school system.

Social Policies Impacting the Poor

How to treat those who have less, those who are in need, those who are unemployed or underemployed, and what role governments should have in assisting such individuals is often a source of debate for politicians in both the U.S. and the U.K. Recent political conflicts within the U.S. have involved policies regarding minimum wage. In February of 2014, President Obama announced that he would use an executive order to raise the minimum wage for federal contractors from $7.25 to $10.10 an hour (Huetteman, 2014). In the fall of 2014, large-scale protests by fast food workers brought the topic of minimum wage to the national stage (Sneed, 2014), and voters in four states approved measures to raise the minimum wage during the 2014 midterm elections (Barro, 2014). Despite these gains, efforts to increase the minimum wage have not gone unopposed. Many business groups lobbied against laws (both at the federal and state level) that would increase the minimum wage and conservative politicians often argue that increases to minimum wage would slow job growth (Sullivan, 2014).

Even if children are unaware of specific debates or policies (such as welfare reform of the late 1990s), legacies left by these arguments may impact them. In 1996, President Bill Clinton signed the Personal Responsibility and Work Opportunity Reconciliation Act, which resulted in significant changes to the way welfare was distributed in the U.S., including increasing expectations for individuals to work and placing limits on the use of welfare support. This law was accompanied by outcry from some Democrats who worried that the change would lead to massive increases in homeless children and families (Wolf, 2006). These worst fears did not come true, and the ten-year anniversary of the legislation involved recognition of some victories, including a decrease in child poverty rates and a decrease in the number of people on welfare (Clinton, 2006). Unfortunately, most of the women who left welfare ended up in low-paying and low-skilled jobs (Wolf, 2006). President Clinton himself asserted that raising the minimum wage was an important next step following welfare reform (Clinton, 2006).

In addition to the direct impact welfare reform had on many families' lives, the political dialogues about welfare policies have had lasting effects on the discourse in the U.S. about families in need. Much of the public discourse during the late 1990s asserted that individuals utilizing welfare were lazy and that punitive reforms were needed (Brown, 2013). This type of stigmatizing discourse about social policies designed to support those in poverty can have detrimental effects on children and adolescents. Stuber and Kronebusch (2004) found that the stigma associated with welfare was so powerful that it often served as a barrier to enrolling in Temporary Assistance to Needy Families (TANF) and Medicaid. Children who hear negative messages about those living in poverty may bully others whose families utilize public assistance programs or may internalize the negative stereotypes about their own families. While some children may question stereotypes about the poor, others may internalize these ideas and reinforce them through their interactions with peers.

Social Class in the Media

Most representations of social class in popular media in the U.S. and the U.K. emphasize class divides and portray stereotypical images in which material wealth is glorified and those living in poverty are often ridiculed. These media representations frequently paint people with broad strokes—making sweeping generalizations about individuals with various amounts of access to wealth, education, and financial power. Such limited depictions can be found in advertising, television, and film. Although stereotypical images appear to be pervasive, some media makers have utilized their genre to examine and critique the current social class structure.

A number of scholars have addressed the ways in which marketers directly target children and adolescents and the potential psychological consequences of this (Brown, Lamb, & Tappan, 2009; Lamb & Brown, 2006). Quart (2003) argues that Generation Y has grown up in a culture that emphasizes name brands as social capitol. This growing emphasis on having the coolest brands of clothes and the latest technological gadgetry can place pressure on children from families who do not have the financial resources to purchase these things. Marketers capitalize on this anxiety and the fear that children will be treated as outcasts to encourage individuals (kids and parents) to buy their products (Quart, 2003). In the back-to-school season of 2013, a television and Internet ad for JC Penny aired in the U.S. that created a stir and outcry from parents who worried that the ad was promoting bullying (Valez, 2013). The ad includes a female voiceover talking about how important it is to get the right brands of clothes. A child sits alone at a table in the cafeteria and the voiceover says, "I've been told that this stuff can make or break an entire year." Many parents argued that the ad—along with some of JC Penny's print ads running during that time—were promoting class-based bullying. The company asserted that they did not intend to promote or trivialize bullying and pulled the ad from network television. Nevertheless, this ad demonstrated the types of pressures that might encourage kids to tease others who do not have the trendiest clothing or accessories.

American media often represents individuals' class situations as resulting from choices those individuals have made—attempting to perpetuate the myth that people can pull themselves up by the bootstraps and rise from rags to riches. Those who live in poverty are commonly portrayed as being products of their own "poor" decisions, with the implication being that they could do better if they just worked harder. The popular U.S.-based reality television show *Here Comes Honey Boo Boo* (Lexton, Rogan, & Reddy, 2012) received mixed reactions for its portrayal of a working-class family (Venutolo, 2012). This reality TV show stared Alana Thompson—aka Honey Boo Boo—a six-year-old girl who participated in child beauty pageants. While some argued that the show was a celebration of working-class families, many critics asserted that the intention of the show was to ridicule and exploit the family (Olen, 2012).

The popular British show *Misfits* (Crowe, 2009) included a number of teenagers who were engaging in community service as punishment for some delinquent behavior. One of the characters, Kelly Bailey, was teased early on in the show and called a *chav*—a pejorative British term used to refer to a "lower-class person typified by brash and loutish behavior and the wearing of (real or imitation) designer clothes" (*Oxford Dictionaries*). While she was teased less as the show continued and the teens built relationships with each other, class-based bullying was not challenged within the show. This representation demonstrated a phenomenon occurring in Britain in which working-class individuals are being portrayed in increasingly negative ways.

Jones (2011) examines the chav stereotype and argues that working-class individuals in Britain have become an object of fear and ridicule.

Other media images highlight school rivalries in which social class is a source of divide and is used to deepen rivalries and justify exclusion, ostracism, and competition. For example, in the film *Bring it On* (Abraham & Bliss, 2000), two high school cheerleading squads attending "rival" schools strive to make it to the national cheerleading competition. Although social class is not explicitly cited as the source of the rivalry, the film typecasts the schools as a poor inner-city school (the Clovers) and a wealthier suburban school (the Toros). The film's plot revolves around the conflict between the two schools as a new cheer captain of the Toros discovers that the previous captain often stole their routines from the Clovers and used those routines at the regional and national competitions. They could only do so because the Clovers were never able to afford to attend the competitions. Such media images likely mirror real cases of schools engaging in rivalries embedded with social-class tension. Class-based bullying can occur in the spaces where schools gather together, including sporting events and competitions of club teams (such as debate).

Although American and British media include numerous examples of class-based stereotypes, some individuals have used their access to the media to attempt to challenge cultural messages about poverty. Tavis Smiley and Cornell West documented the *Poverty Tour* they took through the U.S. in August of 2011 on Smiley's PBS show and in their book (Smiley & West, 2012). The tour was intended to be an opportunity to dialogue with people around the country who were struggling financially and to give people a chance to share their stories. In their book, Smiley and West (2012) commented on the ways communities responded when they arrived in a new location and asked about people living in poverty. They often encountered shame, embarrassment, and resistance. Some insisted that their town didn't have poverty. Some individuals who themselves appeared to be living below the poverty line did not want to be identified as poor. Smiley and West argued that such shame likely resulted from internalized stereotypes about the poor. Their tour was crucial in not only shedding light on people's lived experiences but also in their work to reframe discussions of poverty by emphasizing the dignity of all people and the need to treat everyone with respect. Although it is outnumbered by stereotypical representations of social class, theirs was an important example of the way media can be used to present alternatives to stereotypical images.

LEGAL RIGHTS FOR LGBTQ INDIVIDUALS

Examining the battles for legal rights for the LGBTQ community within the U.S. and the U.K. provide opportunities to understand how attitudes may be transferred from the larger community into a school. Cultural and political debates about legal rights for LGBTQ individuals have entered some schools through controversies about school policies, decisions about curriculum, and arguments about what books to allow in the school library. In some schools, a bias against same-sex parents extends to the literature children read, with educators banning (or expressing a desire to ban) books that feature same-sex parents. For example, *And Tango Makes Three*, a book about gay penguins who adopt an orphaned baby penguin, made the top slot on the American Library Association's 2010 list of most frequently challenged books (Siemaszko, 2011). Critics claim that the book promotes homosexuality and thus is inappropriate for children. Children who are exposed to such negative rhetoric about homosexuality may be more likely to tease, exclude, or otherwise bully children who they perceive to be gay or lesbian or children who have gay/lesbian parents.

Same-Sex Marriage Policies

While there have been a number of important legal areas addressed by LGBTQ advocates (such as antidiscrimination policies and rights for transgender individuals), one of the most widely publicized battles within the U.S. and the U.K. has involved the legal right for same-sex marriage. The political parties in the United Kingdom have generally been more supportive of same-sex marriage than those of the United States, which has been reflected in the public discourse about the issue. Even the Conservative Party within the U.K. was lukewarm on the issue, stating in 2010 that they would consider ending the ban on same-sex marriage (BBC, 2010), with more liberal parties calling for legislation to legalize same-sex marriage as early as 2009 ("LDEG's Antony Hook interviews Nick Clegg," 2009). By contrast, it wasn't until 2012 that President Obama, the leader of the Democratic Party in the U.S., announced that he openly supports same-sex marriage, despite his previous opposition to marriage equality (Gast, 2012).

Throughout the process of writing this book, the legal landscape in the U.S. regarding access to marriage shifted frequently as court cases were decided and new lawsuits arose. Although not exclusively, court decisions predominantly moved in the direction of expanding rights of nonheterosexual individuals. In June 2013, the United States Supreme Court ruled that the Defense of Marriage Act (DOMA) was unconstitutional (Barnes, 2013). This ruling resulted in the federal government providing full legal recognition of married gay couples. As of December 2014, same-sex marriage was legal in 35 states and the District of Columbia (Human Rights Campaign, 2015). Shortly before this book went to press in the summer of 2015, the Supreme Court of the United States ruled that under the 14th Amendment, states must issue marriage licenses to same-sex couples, resulting in nationwide marriage equality. However, these changes to the laws did not happen quietly. In general, most of the states legalized same-sex marriage one at a time (although a few happened on the same day) and most resulted from long court battles. Announcements were often met with fanfare on social media and discussions within mainstream news organizations. Despite the legalization of same-sex marriage in the majority of states, there continues to be vocal opposition. The Republican Party asserts that marriage should be limited to one man and one woman—this belief was included on their official platform in 2014 (Republican National Committee). In addition, numerous individual politicians remain outspoken in their opposition to same-sex marriage. For example, the Arizona Congressman Matt Soloman made a splash in early 2013 during an interview on local Arizona news when he said that despite having a gay son he was not in support of gay marriage (Michalscheck, 2013).

The progression of legalizing same-sex marriage in the United Kingdom was not without challenge but was perhaps less vitriolic than the battles that were waged within the United States. In the summer of 2013, the Parliament of the United Kingdom passed the Marriage (Same Sex Couples) Act, which legalized same-sex marriage in England and Wales. In February of 2014, the Scottish Parliament passed a similar law legalizing same-sex marriage. Northern Ireland remains the sole hold out within the United Kingdom, allowing for civil partnerships but not marriage among same-sex couples. However, the movement toward marriage equality within England, Wales, and Scotland was not without resistance. The main opposition stemmed from religious groups (especially Catholics) who were concerned that churches might one day be forced to provide marriage services to same-sex couples (Heyden & Townsend, 2014).

A "Modern" Family; Media Representations of LGBTQ Individuals

Children are also exposed to discussions about same-sex marriage and LGBT individuals through the media. For example, the 2014 Grammys showcased a large marriage ceremony on stage, including many same-sex couples (Nichols, 2014). In general, media representations of LGBTQ individuals changed drastically in the first decade of the 21st century. For the most part, popular representations of LGBTQ individuals became more complex, positive, and affirming. However, these representations were met with resistance and some shows portrayed increasingly entrenched and stereotyped views of members of the LGBTQ population.

The show *Modern Family* (Levitan et al., 2009), which premiered in 2009 has been credited as helping to shift conversations about gay and lesbian couples. The television show, which airs during prime time on network television in the U.S., portrays what is meant to be the "modern American family" and includes divorced parents of adult children, a father remarried to a younger, Latina woman, and a gay couple. The sitcom focuses on day-to-day life for the family members as they navigate their relationships with each other, pressures at work, and the challenges of raising families. Although there is occasional reference to the father having previously struggled when his son came out, the gay couple is accepted as part of the family. This couple goes on to adopt a child and later to get married. According to a poll by *The Hollywood Reporter* (Appelo, 2012), watching *Modern Family* and similar shows that featured openly gay characters led to increased support for gay marriage among Americans. In fact, 42% of the individuals in their poll indicated that seeing gay marriage on television made them more aware of and active in regard to political issues related to gay marriage. However, this same poll also showed that a small portion of viewers (6%) became more opposed to gay marriage as a result of television shows that included gay characters. Other television shows have also highlighted some of the continued opposition to same-sex marriage within the U.S. In late 2013, a controversy broke out when the star of the reality TV show *Duck Dynasty* (Gurney, Gurney, Bryant, & Neumeyer, 2012) made numerous negative comments about the LGBTQ community, including saying that being gay is a sin (Sieczkowski, 2013). His comments added fuel to the fire of the already burning controversy surrounding same-sex marriage and antidiscrimination laws.

The Transgender Community

The momentum that has gathered around securing same-sex marriage rights within the U.K. and the U.S. has been notable. Many families in both countries have been significantly impacted by increased access to the legal rights and protections that accompany marriage. Now that same-sex marriage is legal within the U.S. and most of the U.K., it is important for LGBTQ advocates to consider how to build on this momentum to address other important issues facing this population. One area of growing cultural awareness concerns transgender, intersex, and gender nonconforming individuals. Popular television shows such as *Orange Is the New Black* (Kohan, 2013) and *Transparent* (Soloway, 2014) feature transgender characters. While these characters' story lines include exploration of topics related to being transgender (such as transitioning, interfacing with the medical community, and experiences of discrimination and rejection from community members), they also are integrated into the larger plotlines. While these shows represent only a small fraction of the experiences within the transgender community, they are contributing to a growing cultural awareness.

IMMIGRATION, ETHNICITY, AND RELIGION

While it is important to recognize that ethnicity, country of origin, and religion are not synonymous, many of the cultural discussions related to these three aspects of identity often conflate them. In this chapter, I highlight a few examples of ways that cultural tensions related to immigration, ethnicity, or religion can make their way into schools and into the interactions between children. There are some commonalities in the U.S. and the U.K. regarding racial-based bullying (including identity-based bullying against Muslim children or children of Arab descent). There are also patterns of identity-based bullying unique to each country, which highlights the impact of geopolitical issues upon children and their interactions with each other. First, I explore how the war on terror has impacted children within the United States and the United Kingdom. Next, I examine how the election of the first Black president of the United States sparked discussions of racial relations both within and outside of schools. Finally, I demonstrate how the historical religious and sociopolitical tensions within Northern Ireland often play out in the schoolyard. It is important to note that these are not the only relevant examples. For example, children within the United States are likely impacted by heated conversations and debates about immigration from Mexico, Central America, and South America. As the cultural dialogues about various aspects of ethnicity, nationality, and religion shift, the influence of these factors on children's interactions may change. Educators can be aware of and recognize such potential impacts and do more to engage their students in antiracist dialogues that may deter identity-based bullying.

The War on Terror

Within the U.S., the terrorist attack that occurred on September 11, 2001 impacted conversations within the country regarding immigration policies and terrorism. As the U.S. entered two wars in the Middle East (one in Afghanistan, the other in Iraq) that spanned more than a decade, many children likely grew up hearing negative messages about individuals from this region of the world. Even more than a decade after 9/11, children are exposed to anti-Arab sentiments that may influence their treatment of Arab or Muslim children. For example, in the fall of 2013, the first Miss America of Indian descent was crowned. The announcement of Nina Davuluri as the winner was met with numerous vitriolic responses on social media (Golgowski, 2013). Many accused her of not being American, of being a foreigner, and some even called her a terrorist. Sadly, these reactions appear to mirror many children's experiences of identity-based bullying on the basis of their nationality, religion, or ethnicity. Some reports by advocacy groups indicated that bullying of Muslim children increased as a result of post-9/11 Islamophobia (Holcomb, 2011; Sacirbey, 2011). Even children who are not Muslim have been targeted with anti-Islam bullying. A 2014 survey found that half of the Sikh children surveyed reported experiencing bullying in schools, and if the children wore turbans to school the number rose to two-thirds (De Bode, 2014). Many of these children were teased, called *terrorists*, or even experienced physical violence, including being hit, kicked, or having their turbans taken from their heads.

The United Kingdom has also been impacted by the terrorist attack on 9/11 and the subsequent wars in the Middle East. Negative rhetoric about

Muslims may contribute to the experiences of identity-based bullying faced by Muslim and/or Arab children in the United Kingdom. A report by ChildLine indicated a disturbing increase in racist bullying and reported that in 2013, over 1,400 children sought counseling after such experiences (Gunaratnam, 2014). Muslim children in particular were often targeted with identity-based bullying and were called names like *bomber* and *terrorist*. While some of the identity-based bullying appears to apply specifically to Muslim children, there is a broader reach of anti-immigration sentiments. Ruck and Tenenbaum (2014) found that in a study of youth in the U.K., immigrant and asylum-seeking youth were more vulnerable to intergroup exclusion than majority youth.

Post-Racial America?

Issues of ethnicity within the U.S. were complicated by the election of the nation's first African American president. Some wondered whether this election meant the United States had entered an age of a "post-racial America" (Schorr, 2008), wherein discussions of ethnicity and racism were no longer necessary. Certainly some research indicates there were many positive impacts of the election, especially for Black/African American youth. Fuller-Rowell, Burrow, and Ong (2011) found that African American college students increased in their identity exploration following the election of Obama in 2008. In particular, African American college students' racial identities became more salient and more positive as a result of their perceived shift in group status. While this study focused on college students, the mean age was 19.3, just slightly older than high school students. It is probable that high school students were also impacted by the presidential election, both in terms of thinking about their own identity as well as the identities of others.

Although I am hopeful that the long overdue election of a non-White president will help to continue to dismantle racism within the United States, I think it is overly optimistic (and perhaps naive) to assume this is indicative of a post-racial America. In fact, numerous political commentators have noted that throughout his presidency, Obama has received criticism that appears to be rooted in racism. Former President Jimmy Carter commented on some of the attacks that were made against President Obama saying, "I think people who are guilty of that kind of personal attack against Obama have been influenced to a major degree by a belief that he should not be president because he happens to be African American" (CNN, 2009). More research is needed to understand whether racially based bullying (particularly against African American children) increased, decreased, or remained constant during this time. Nonetheless, school administrators should consider the implications of larger cultural conversations about race relations within the U.S. on the dynamics playing out within their individual schools.

Religion and Bullying in Northern Ireland

Within the United Kingdom, issues of culture and religion at times become conflated, in particular in struggles within Northern Ireland. Although tensions decreased during the last decade of the 20th century, the battles within Northern Ireland resulted in numerous policy decisions and cultural consequences. While the conflict in Northern Ireland is primarily about political freedom (whether Northern Ireland is controlled by England or part of the Independent Republic of Ireland), the history of the conflict included religious tension between Catholics and Protestants. This tension influenced the development of segregated schools and has impacted children in Northern Ireland in direct and indirect ways. In 1922, a committee of representatives from the Protestant Church released the Lynn Report, which documented their recommendations for a national school system for Northern Ireland (Green, 2001). The Lynn Report recommended that religious education in schools should be open to all religions, but in practice the education was Protestant. The Education Act of 1930 then made the religious divide official with state schools being fully funded and Protestant and voluntary schools being Catholic and funded only at 50% (Green, 2001). It was not until 50 years later, with the passage of the Education Reform Act of 1989, that there was a systemic attempt to address sectarian divisions in schools. It called for official support for integrated schools (integrating both students and teachers) and to develop mechanisms for Catholics to influence educational policy (Green, 2001). Despite such reform attempts, the schools in Northern Ireland continue to be mostly divided by religion—in 2012, 90% of children attended Catholic schools or state (Protestant) schools (Borooah & Knox, 2013).

Although efforts have increased to integrate schools, the long history of division has contributed to the development of prejudices and stereotypes (Hughes, 2011). In the long run, having more children attend integrated schools will hopefully serve to improve relationships among Catholics and Protestants in Northern Ireland and to help heal decades of wounds and political tensions. However, as children begin to attend integrated schools, it is likely that students will play out the historical strife in the form of identity-based bullying against children perceived to be outsiders. School administrators can be intentional about addressing the legacies of conflict and prejudices that children may bring with them into integrated schools to detect and prevent identity-based bullying for today's children and help heal a nation for the future.

CONCLUSION

It was challenging to choose only a few examples of the connections between larger social forces and children's engagement in identity-based bullying and there are many more that could be examined. While it is important to analyze the specific influences on any one aspect of identity-based bullying, an essential step for scholars, advocates, and school officials focused on anti-bullying work is to acknowledge that such parallels do exist. All too often when individuals identify the "causes" of bullying, the focus remains on individual characteristics, pathology, and unique interpersonal conflicts between children. While I am not advocating that those factors be dismissed, I stress the value of examining the larger social causes. John Donne wrote in his seventeenth devotion, *Meditation XVII*, "No man is an island." Sometimes it seems that we forget that no child is an island, either. Perhaps this oversight results from our adult desires to guard children from the worst of society's influences. Ignoring that these effects exist does not protect children; rather, it allows us to forgo opportunities to create interventions that account for these factors, which may be the key to creating deep and lasting social change.

REFERENCES

Abraham, M., & Bliss, T. A. (Producers), & Reed, P. (Director). (2000). *Bring it on* [Motion picture]. United States: Beacon Communications.

Appelo, T. (2012, November 3). THR poll: 'Glee' and 'Modern Family' drive voters to favor gay marriage—even many Romney voters. *The Hollywood Reporter.* Retrieved from http://www.hollywoodreporter.com/news/thr-poll-glee-modern-family-386225

Barnes, R. (2013, June 26). Supreme court strikes down key part of Defense of Marriage Act. *The Washington Post.* Retrieved from http://www.washingtonpost.com/politics/supreme-court/2013/06/26/f0039814-d9ab-11e2-a016-92547bf094cc_story.html

Barro, J. (2014, November 3). Four states vote to raise the minimum wage. *The New York Times.* Retrieved from http://www.nytimes.com/2014/11/05/upshot/election-results-2014-minimum-wage.html?_r=0&abt=0002&abg=0

BBC. (2010, April 11). George Osborne says Tories will 'consider gay marriage'. *BBC.* Retrieved from *http://news.bbc.co.uk/2/hi/uk_news/politics/election_2010/8614235.stm*

Borooah, V., & Knox, C. (2013). The contribution of 'shared education' to Catholic-Protestant reconciliation in Northern Ireland: A third way? *British Educational Research Journal, 39,* 925–946. doi: 10.1002/berj.3017

Brown, H. (2013). The new racial politics of welfare: Ethno-racial diversity, immigration, and welfare discourse variation. *Social Service Review, 87,* 586–612.

Brown, L. M., Lamb, S., & Tappan, M. (2009). *Packaging boyhood: Saving our sons from superheroes, slackers and other media stereotypes.* New York, NY: St. Martin's Press.

Chav. (n.d.). In *Oxford Dictionaries online.* Retrieved from http://www.oxforddictionaries.com/definition/english/chav?q=chav

Clinton, B. (2006, August 22). How we ended welfare, together. *The New York Times.* Retrieved from http://www.nytimes.com/2006/08/22/opinion/22clinton.html?_r=0

CNN. (2009, September 17). Carter again cites racism as factor in Obama's treatment. *CNN Politics.* Retrieved from http://www.cnn.com/2009/POLITICS/09/15/carter.obama/index.html?eref=ib_us

Crowe, K. (Producer). (2009). *Misfits* [Television series]. London, England: Clerkenwell Films.
De Bode, L. (2014, March 13). 'Go home, terrorist': Sokh children bullied twice the national average. *Aljazeera America*. Retrieved from http://america.aljazeera.com/articles/2014/3/13/a-go-home-terroristasikhchildrenbulliedtwicenationalaverage.html
Fuller-Rowell, T. E., Burrow, A. L., & Ong, A. D. (2011). Changes in racial identity among African American college students following the election of Barack Obama. *Developmental Psychology, 47*, 1608–1618.
Gast, P. (2012, May 9). Obama announces he supports same-sex marriage. *CNN*. Retrieved from http://www.cnn.com/2012/05/09/politics/obama-same-sex-marriage/
Golgowski, N. (2013, September 16). Miss America crowns first winner of Indian descent, and critics slam her as Arab terrorist. *New York Daily News*. Retrieved from http://www.nydailynews.com/news/national/1st-america-indian-descent-slammed-arab-article-1.1457133
Green, J. E. (2001). *Education in the United Kingdom and Ireland (Studies in education)*. Bloomington, IN: Phi Delta Kappa International.
Gunaratnam, Y. (2014, January 31). How should we prepare our children for racism? *The Independent*. Retrieved from http://research.gold.ac.uk/9872/1/how-should-we-prepare-our-children-for-racism-9067230.html
Gurney, D., Gurney, S., Bryant, E. F., Neumeyer, L. (Producers). (2012). *Duck dynasty* [Television series]. Monroe, LA: Gurney Productions.
Heyden, T., & Townsend, L. (2014, March 26). The people who oppose the gay marriage law. *BBC News Magazine*. Retrieved from http://www.bbc.com/news/magazine-26634214
Holcomb, S. (2011, December 3). Muslims in America: When bullying meets religion. *Muslim Matters*. Retrieved from http://muslimmatters.org/2011/12/13/muslims-in-america-when-bullying-meets-religion/
Huetteman, E. (2014, July 15). Obama calls for minimum wage rise and equal pay as elections approach. *The New York Times*. Retrieved from http://www.nytimes.com/2014/09/02/us/politics/obama-takes-to-road-to-push-rise-in-minimum-wage.html?_r=0
Hughes, J. (2011). Are separate schools divisive? A case study from Northern Ireland. *British Educational Research Journal, 37*, 829–850. doi: 10.1080/01411926.2010.506943Jones, O. (2011). *Chavs: The demonization of the working class*. London, England: Verso.
Klein, J. (2006). Cultural capital and high school bullies: How social inequality impacts school violence. *Men and Masculinities, 9*, 53–75. doi: 10.1177/1097184X04271387
Kohan, J. (Creator). (2013). *Orange is the New Black* [Television series]. USA. Lionsgate Television.
Lamb, S., & Brown, L. M. (2006). *Packaging girlhood: Rescuing our daughters from marketers' schemes*. New York, NY: St. Martin's Griffin.
LDEG's Antony Hook interviews Nick Clegg MP. (2009, September 17). *Liberal democrat European group*. Retrieved from http://ldeg.org/en/article/2009/0097502/ldeg-s-antony-hook-interviews-nick-clegg-mp
Levitan, S., Lloyd, C., Morton, J., Corrigan, P., O'Shannon, D., Walsh, B, . . . Higginbotham, A. (Producers). (2009). *Modern family* [Television series]. Los Angeles, CA: Lloyd-Levitan Productions.
Lexton, L., Rogan, T., & Reddy, S. (Producers). (2012). *Here comes Honey Boo Boo* [Television series]. Burbank, CA: Authentic Entertainment.
Liu, W. M., Soleck, G., Hopps, J., Dunston, K., & Pickett, T. (2004). A new framework to understand social class in counseling: The social class worldview and

modern classism theory. *Journal of Multicultural Counseling and Development, 32*, 95–122. doi: 10.1002/j.2161-1912.2004.tb00364.x

Michalscheck, A. (2013, March 29). Gay son doesn't change congressman's view on gay marriage. *AZFamily.com*. Retrieved from http://www.azfamily.com/news/Gay-son-doesnt-change-congressmans-view-on-gay-marriage-200686251.html

Nichols, J. (2014, January 27). Anti-gay pundits freak out over Grammys gay wedding ceremony. *The Huffington Post*. Retrieved from http://www.huffingtonpost.com/2014/01/27/same-sex-wedding-grammys_n_4674469.html

Olen, H. (2012, September 9). Honey Boo Boo: Dwarf tossing for the reality age. *Forbes*. Retrieved from http://www.forbes.com/sites/helaineolen/2012/09/26/honey-boo-boo-dwarf-tossing-for-the-reality-show-age/

Peachey, J., Smith, N., & Sharma, N. (December, 2013). *Families in need of food parcels—The food poverty crisis unwrapped*. Barnardo's Strategy Unit, 1–23. Retrieved from http://www.barnardos.org.uk/resources/research_and_publications/families-in-need-of-food-parcels/publication-view.jsp?pid=PUB-2220

Quart, A. (2003). *Branded: The buying and selling of teenagers*. New York, NY: Basic Books.

Republican National Committee. (n.d.). *Republican Platform*. Retrieved from https://www.gop.com/platform/renewing-american-values/

Ruck, M. D., & Tenenbaum, H. R. (2014). Does moral and social conventional reasoning predict British young people's judgments about the rights of asylum-seeking youth? *Journal of Social Issues, 70*, 47–62.

Sacirbey, O. (2011, September, 8). 9/11 Bullying: Muslim teens push back. *Huffington Post*. Retrieved from http://www.huffingtonpost.com/2011/09/07/bullying-muslim-teens-push-back_n_952947.html

Schorr, D. (2008, January 28). A new 'post-racial' political era in America. *National Public Radio*. Retrieved from http://www.npr.org/templates/story/story.php?storyId=18489466

Sieczkowski, C. (2013, December 18). 'Duck Dynasty' star Phil Robertson makes anti-gay remarks, says being gay is a sin. *Huffington Post*. Retrieved from http://www.huffingtonpost.com/2013/12/18/duck-dynasty-phil-robertson-gay_n_4465564.html

Siemaszko, C. (2011, April 13). Ban 'And Tango Makes Three'?: Book about gay penguins ops 'most challenged' list-again. *Daily News*. Retrieved from http://www.nydailynews.com/news/national/ban-tango-book-gay-penguins-tops-challenged-list-article-1.115499

Smiley, T., & West, C. (2012). *The rich and the rest of us: A poverty manifesto*. New York, NY: Smiley Books.

Sneed, T. (2014, September 3). Fast-food workers to strike to super-size their wages: The workers want a pay raise, and politicians are listening. *U.S. News and World Report*. Retrieved from http://www.usnews.com/news/articles/2014/09/03/fast-food-restaurant-strike-plays-into-larger-minimum-wage-battle

Soloway, J. (Creator). (2014). *Transparent* [Television series]. USA: Picrow.

Stuber, J., & Kronebusch, K. (2004). Stigma and other determinants of participation in TANF and Medicaid. *Journal of Policy Analysis and Management, 23*, 509–530. doi: 10.1002/pam.20024

Sullivan, A. (2014, September 15). Minimum wage hike finds hope in U.S. heartland. *The Huffington Post*. Retrieved from http://www.huffingtonpost.com/2014/09/15/minimum-wage-hike_n_5821406.html

Valez, M. (2013, August 14). J.C. Penney back-to-school ad 'promotes bullying,' parents say. *The Huffington Post*. Retrieved from http://www.huffingtonpost.com/2013/08/14/jcpenney-back-to-school-ad_n_3756517.html

Venutolo, A. (2012, August 9). Here comes Honey Boo Boo: Revolting or amusing? Or revoltingly amusing? *The Star Ledger.* Retrieved from http://www.nj.com/entertainment/tv/index.ssf/2012/08/here_comes_honey_boo_boo_tlc_v.html

Wolf, R. (2006, July 18). How welfare reform changed America. *USA Today.* Retrieved from http://usatoday30.usatoday.com/news/nation/2006-07-17-welfare-reform-cover_x.htm

5 Educational Structures and Policies Impacting Identity-Based Bullying

Although identity-based bullying can take place in any setting, in this book I focus predominantly on schools. The reason for this is twofold. First, many incidents of bullying occur in schools and these events have detrimental effects on children and their ability to receive an education. Second, schools can be sources of programing to prevent and intervene in identity-based bullying. In this chapter, I explore how educational structures—as well as policies and laws about bullying, education, and discrimination—affect identity-based bullying in schools. I highlight key similarities and differences in these factors between the United States and the United Kingdom and demonstrate how these issues may impact the way these countries approach identity-based bullying. First, I provide a brief description of some of the key educational structures of the United States and the United Kingdom, including how policies are made. Next, I explore educational reforms that can indirectly impact attempts to address identity-based bullying. These include the No Child Left Behind program in the United States (Jennings & Rentner, 2006) and the rise of free schools and high-stakes testing in the United Kingdom (Smith, 2012). I examine policies/laws regarding bullying in schools and policies/laws regarding protection of children based on aspects of their identity. Finally, I explore the importance of the climate of a school and how it can impact identity-based bullying.

STRUCTURE OF EDUCATION IN THE U.S. AND U.K.

The structures of schools and school systems can lend themselves to either promote or deter identity-based bullying and shape the way that policies are written, programming decisions are made, and interventions are implemented. As discussed in Chapter 3, many scholars have argued that most schooling in the western world is conceptualized in such a way that inequality is reinforced and maintained. The structures of these systems often function to systematize the privileging of some identities over others. Understanding how educational systems are designed is essential to exploring both the creation of the problem of identity-based bullying as well as effective solutions. In this chapter, I will not cover all there is to know about the structure of education in the United States and the United Kingdom, but I do provide an overview of the structures, as well as the history of reforms, to offer a framework for understanding how schooling works. I encourage readers who are unfamiliar with either system to seek out additional resources (for example, Green, 2001; Rury, 2012; Smith, 2012).

The United States

The educational system in the United States is directly impacted by the fact that the national government consists of a federation of states. This means that power over schooling is distributed among federal, state, and local decision makers, resulting in numerous differences in education from one region to the next. There are some general aspects of the educational structure that are mostly consistent across the nation. First, Americans are provided with free education in kindergarten through twelfth grade (K–12) in the form of public schools. However, some families elect to send children to private schools. School districts focus on schooling in K–12 (sometimes including pre-K), while post–high school education is managed separately. While there are exceptions, most school districts split up schooling into three separate systems based on grades. Elementary schools consist of kindergarten through fifth or sixth grade (approximate ages 5–11), middle schools or junior highs consist of sixth through eighth or seventh through ninth grades (approximate ages 12–14), and high schools consist of ninth or tenth through twelfth grades (approximate ages 15–18). Many states originally divided schooling into only two categories (elementary school and high school). In 1909, the Ohio Board of Education created the first junior high school in the country with the hopes that it would better prepare students for the rigor of high school and decrease dropout rates (Ohio History Connection, 2013), and most other states followed suit.

Funding for the public K–12 school system is provided by federal, state, and local governments. As of 2010, funding from the federal government composed about 10% of school budgets, while 90% originated from a combination of state and local sources (Ravitch, 2010). Access to federal funding is often used to encourage compliance with federal educational guidelines and schools that do not follow these guidelines may lose funding (for example, see the discussions that follow regarding the No Child Left Behind policy and funding for the Race to the Top Program). Schools receive a large percentage of their budgets from the state, but there are significant differences in the amount of money that is dedicated to K–12 schools from state to state. There are also discrepancies in school quality from state to state. Finally, school systems receive funding through local governments, often in the form of property taxes based on the value of homes in an area. Generally, the more a home is worth, the more money a homeowner pays in property taxes. This means that schools located in neighborhoods with higher property values get more funding than schools located in neighborhoods where the houses are worth less. This system perpetuates inequalities because neighborhoods with higher property values also have schools that receive more funding than schools in neighborhoods with a lower tax base (e.g., more rental properties and less expensive homes).

Educational policies within the U.S. are made at every level of government. While the federal government mandates some policies through federal laws and policies made by the Department of Education (established in 1867 to assist states in developing school systems), state and local governments are also entitled to make laws concerning education. These laws can span everything from topic areas taught (or banned from being taught), programming that is required, and curriculum training needed for teachers to be certified within a given state. School policies are also heavily influenced by local school boards, which are composed of individuals elected or appointed to represent the community. While school boards are mandated to follow federal and state educational laws, they make many of the decisions about how these laws are interpreted and implemented, as well as assessing various school programs (Center for Public Education, n.d.). As a result of these multiple layers of funding and decision making, educational policies and practices regarding identity-based bullying vary widely from one school district to the next.

The United Kingdom

Understanding the school system in the U.K. requires recognizing that the United Kingdom is composed of multiple countries with similarities and differences in regard to culture in general and educational structures and values in particular. Here I will summarize some key points about the ways in which education is structured, in particular exploring how policies are made within and outside of schools, (see Green, 2001 for additional details). The educational system in England and Wales is centralized and communication and policy decisions are mostly overseen by the Office for Standards in Education (OFSTED). The OFSTED evaluates education being offered and reviews the spiritual, moral, social, and cultural development of students. Northern Ireland and Scotland retain some independence in their educational system, although they are heavily influenced by the educational procedures and policies utilized in England and Wales.

England is the most populated country within the United Kingdom and until 1870 lacked any government-supported schools. In 1870, the Foster Act divided England into school districts, which allowed local school boards to collect taxes in order to support schools. In 1918, elementary education became free for all children. In 1944, the Butler Act created a Ministry of Education and made education free and compulsory until the age of 15. The Education Reform Act of 1988 created a national curriculum council and allowed for the development of grant-maintained schools. Local education agencies (LEAs) oversee the operation of these state maintained schools. Independent schools have to register with the LEAs but are mostly free from government control. Schools receive about half of their funding through a local council and the other half from the national government.

Before the Education Reform Act of 1988, the curriculum in U.K. schools was determined primarily by head teachers. The act created a national curriculum and testing standards for England and Wales. The national curriculum is rather detailed and includes a complex system of implementation and assessment, with students being required to take examinations at the end of compulsory schooling. Some students remain in school for an extra year to prepare for university and take an extra exam upon completion. The national curriculum was extended to Northern Ireland, but Scotland's education system remains independent. Many educational experts around the world consider Scotland to have the best educational system in the U.K. (Green, 2001). Education Scotland was formed in 2011 as the public body responsible for education within Scotland, and it currently oversees educational policies and curriculum decisions.

REFORM MOVEMENTS

Numerous school reforms have been attempted in the U.S. and the U.K., which have a variety of implications on equity within schools. Within the U.S., concerns about the educational system have been part of the cultural milieu at least since the publishing of the *Coleman Report* in 1966 (Ravitch, 2010). This report indicated that there were disparities in educational achievement among individuals from various ethnic and socioeconomic backgrounds. It also examined achievement of U.S. students in subjects such as math, science, and reading and compared them to international data. Such comparisons indicated that the U.S. was behind other developed nations in some areas of educational attainment. In 1983, the report *A Nation at Risk* (sponsored by the National Commission on Excellence in Education), was released and furthered American concerns about educational outcomes. The report made recommendations that schools in the U.S. adopt specific curricular and programmatic changes in order to improve the quality of education provided to all children in the nation. Ravitch (2010) argues that this report played an important role in raising Americans' awareness about the need for educational reform. However, the report was not accompanied by a federal mandate or the adoption of federal laws, so individual states were left to decide whether or not they wanted to adopt the recommendations within the report. Despite the lack of a mechanism to enforce the recommendations, the publishing of this report appeared to spur on a movement toward developing national curriculum standards.

Unfortunately, the initial drafts of the standards for history (one of the first subjects addressed) were met with criticism, as some felt they were too "political" in their representation because they included women, people of color, and the history of oppression within the U.S. (Ravitch, 2010). The standards were soon dubbed too controversial and leaders on both the political right and left distanced themselves from them. By extension, most politicians refused to support any specific curriculum standards and the momentum that had been pulling the country in the direction of a unified approach to education slowed to a halt. The specific critique of the history standards is especially disturbing and reveals assumptions implicit in some expectations about education. Examining these assumptions elucidates one of the ways in which educational systems can reinforce the perspectives of those in the majority. The reaction that including women and people of color within history texts was deemed a "political" move implies that history books that emphasize the experiences of white men are somehow apolitical. Such a critique is a crucial example of the way that the experiences of white men are often treated as the norm. Such viewpoints promote the status quo and block discussions of diversity, power, and privilege within American schools.

School of Choice and Charter Schools

One reform seen in both the U.S. and the U.K. involved the creation of school choice policies. These policies produced a more open form of enrollment into public schools. Proponents of school choice often argue that providing individuals with choices about where their children go to school will create incentives for schools to improve so they can attract students. Some have argued that these policies will be particularly beneficial for children living in disadvantaged areas and that schools may even develop niche markets to better educate underserved children (Hoxby, 2002). In practice, most of the time schools have some exclusionary policies that may counter goals of increasing educational equity (Lubienski, Gulosino, & Weitzel, 2009). School of choice policies have faced extensive criticism based on a number of concerns, including such exclusionary practices. Some have questioned whether there is reasonable access to "better" schools, even if the choice to attend them exists. For example, one study in England examined the number of students attending the school closest to them versus traveling in order to attend their school of choice (Burgess, Briggs, McConnell, & Slater, 2006). They found that the majority of pupils in urban areas had a number of schools within five kilometers of where they lived, while less than half of students in rural areas had even one school within that distance, suggesting that the idea of *choice* may vary depending upon where children live. In the U.S., school choice policies typically increase segregation within schools rather than increasing opportunities for disadvantaged children (Taylor, 2009). Because the highest performing public schools are often in greater demand than they can accommodate, many school systems utilize a lottery system, during which hundreds of students vie for limited available slots in a high performing school. This lottery system reinforces the myth of the "American dream"—that anyone can get a chance at success and the right opportunities. The system creates false hope for children who live in districts where schools are underfunded and underperforming. Instead of changing all schools to assure that a quality education is the norm for all children, the lottery system creates an illusion that anyone could potentially rise out of their circumstances if they are lucky enough and work hard enough.

Within the United States, charter schools have arisen as one outcome of school of choice policies. Charter schools are schools that receive public funding but operate independently of public school districts. They often are formed by groups of parents who want children in a given area to be provided with an education unlike what they would receive in public schools. Charter schools at times have more flexibility than public schools to implement creative and innovative programming (Weber, 2010). They may offer specialized education or curriculum in areas such as environmental education or international education. Some charter schools may be more willing than public schools to address identity-based bullying through systemic and targeted programming. In my own experience, I collaborated with a charter school to provide students a social justice educational program. This particular charter school emphasized educating for social equality and the administrators were interested in ways to add to their curriculum. I had reached out to many schools in the area, offering to provide an experiential program teaching students about diversity. This charter school was interested in integrating the workshops into their anti-bullying program, and I was able to adapt the curriculum to address identity-based bullying. As a result, their anti-bullying campaign included training about social justice and integrated conversations about race/ethnicity, gender, and social class (see Brinkman & Manning, 2015). In this case, the charter school was able to provide social justice programming that was not being offered elsewhere in the district. However, charter schools do not have uniform values or consistent expectations, thus some charter schools may actually be the most resistant to such programming. Some scholars have suggested that charter schools may be hesitant to enroll a diverse student body and English language learners for fear that their test numbers will suffer (Ravitch, 2010). Numerous studies have examined the impact of charter schools, often resulting in mixed findings in that some charter schools produce outstanding results while others are severely failing in their task to educate children (Ravitch, 2010).

High-Stakes Testing

Perhaps the largest and (arguably most influential) educational reform movements in the past few decades within the United States and the United

Kingdom have involved policies that resulted in increased use of high-stakes testing. Such policies are of particular interest for the present work because of their potential impact on the types of curriculum offered within schools. High-stakes testing policies are those that attach large consequences to the results of tests (typically standardized and mass-produced tests). While these consequences may apply to the tester (the student) in the form of admission to schools or programs, most of the high-stakes testing policies that have influenced educational systems in the U.S. and the U.K. place consequences on the teachers, administrators, and schools. As a result, these policies put specific demands on schools to ensure that students are prepared to do well on the tests, often resulting in decreased resources available for topics not explicitly tested.

The No Child Left Behind (NCLB) Act was the most recent large-scale reform attempt that was passed at the federal level in the United States (see Ravitch, 2010 and others for a thorough explanation of this act). NCLB focused on making structural changes to schools and emphasized accountability (Ravitch, 2010). It did not include standards for curriculum and focused on testing only in two educational areas (math and reading). The policy was designed to measure schools and then either punish or reward them based on the results. No Child Left Behind included several key features in its accountability plan. A few of these features are particularly important to understand in the context of how the act has impacted identity-based bullying in schools. The act required public schools that received federal funding to test all students in grades 3–8 annually and once in high school. Schools were expected to make adequate yearly progress (AYP), where they moved toward a goal of 100% proficiency in math and reading. Schools not making progress toward proficiency in these subjects faced a series of increasingly severe consequences, including possible curriculum changes, staff changes, and even massive restructuring that could result in firing all the staff or closing the school.

Many have argued that the severe consequences of failure to meet AYP (including the threat of losing one's job) placed pressure on teachers and administrators to focus on teaching math and reading, to teach to the test, and to push out time that could be dedicated to other subjects that would support civic development and awareness of diversity issues (Farnen, 2007; Kellner & Share, 2005). Generally, NCLB did not raise reading and writing levels as much as expected and resulted in fewer resources being dedicated to other types of programming in schools (Weber, 2010). The full extent of the impact of high-stakes testing on curriculum decisions is challenging to determine. One metasynthesis of 49 qualitative studies conducted within the U.S. about the effects of high-stakes testing on schools resulted in somewhat contradictory trends (Au, 2007). In some cases, schools actually expanded their curriculum and used more student-centered approaches. However, most of the time, schools narrowed the curriculum and increased time spent on material that would be on the tests, even at the expense of other subjects. Even if schools saw a value in teaching about identity and diversity and wanted to provide programming that could decrease the incidence of identity-based bullying, the need to focus on test scores often outweighed that desire.

In the United Kingdom, there have been many concerns raised about the increase of testing within schools and the potential impact these exams have on teachers' approach to education. Some assert that the rise of high-stakes testing and emphasis on a national curriculum in Great Britain placed pressure on schools to utilize their time to teach particular subjects and not others. These policies may have stifled the creativity and spontaneity of teachers (Marley, 2008). This is especially troubling because flexibility within the curriculum allows a teacher to turn an incident of identity-based bullying into a teachable moment or to integrate current events into their curriculum to teach their students about social issues. Rigid systems where teachers feel compelled to "teach to the test" can make it challenging for schools to engage in work that would effectively deter identity-based bullying. Emphasis on this form of testing can send the message to students that the goal of education is to learn to please or outsmart other testers rather than to become an engaged democratic citizen.

Common Core

As a result of much criticism of NCLB, many educators within the U.S. sought to renew the movement toward national standards for curriculum. This recent trend has become known as the *Common Core* movement. In contrast to NCLB, Common Core was initiated by the states, with the intention of creating a set of key ideas and skills that students were expected to learn at various educational stages (Murphy, 2014). The idea was that states would choose to adopt the Common Core standards and could utilize tests that would be consistent across state lines. The Obama administration provided an incentive for states to join by offering them an opportunity to access funding through the *Race to the Top* Program. In 2009, governors in 48 states agreed to participate in the development of the new standards. Porter, McMaken, Hwang, and Yang (2011) provided an assessment of the standards for English and mathematics—examining how the Common Core standards compared to existing state standards. Despite support from many academics for the new core, momentum for the movement slowed as critics began to speak out about the new approach. Some conservatives argued that the "common" part of the project represents too much federal oversight of education that should remain in the hands of local authorities (despite the fact that the standards have no federal regulation). Others have expressed concern about the amount and type of testing that has occurred within schools to accompany the adoption of the new standards. The outcry has become politicized, and supporters and the opposition are becoming more and more divided on party lines (although not entirely so). As of the writing of this chapter, about half of the states were still committed to implementing the Common Core, but it seems doubtful that the movement will regain momentum.

A New Vision for Reform

In the United States and the United Kingdom, educational reform movements may be well intentioned in their goals of creating a more educated populace. However, they often distract the public from addressing the potential role that schools could play in creating a more just society. Debates about charter schools, vouchers, academies, and high-stakes testing may keep teachers, administrators, and the public from having much needed conversations about the ways schools are (re)producing inequalities and the high rates of identity-based bullying taking place. Reform movements have most often emphasized achieving better test results in relationship to other nations, increasing math and reading literacy, or changing the ways that schools are funded. Although individual educators and activists have spoken out about shifting the status quo, mainstream movements for educational reform rarely discuss (let alone intend to tackle) inequity in education or challenge traditional notions of the role of schooling within a society. True educational reform should start with a societal evaluation of our goals for our educational institutions. What do we want them to teach? Do we care only about students learning math and reading or should schools play a role in character development? The development of civic responsibility? Learning a sense of fairness and equality? It is possible for schools to be social hubs for justice, but that is not currently the expectation that most people have for their children's educations. Why not?

LAWS AND POLICIES IMPACTING IDENTITY-BASED BULLYING

Laws that apply either directly or indirectly to identity-based bullying impact the way schools conceptualize, prevent, and manage such behavior. It is important for teachers, school administrators, parents, and mental health professionals to be knowledgeable about these laws and what they cover. Schools may or may not respond to identity-based bullying in ways that are consistent with these laws. Their own school-based policies also likely impact how teachers and administrators respond. In the U.S., federal laws prohibit sexual harassment and discrimination based on sex, race, color, and national origin. As of the writing of this book, some states have enacted laws prohibiting bullying of any kind, but these laws are not consistent. In the United Kingdom, there is not one unified legal definition of bullying, but there are laws that apply to bullying in general, as well as identity-based bullying specifically.

Laws in the United States

In the United States there are a number of federal laws that protect students from mistreatment based on various aspects of their identity. Title IX stipulates that no one shall be excluded from or denied the benefits of education on the basis of their sex. Although many think about Title IX as it applies to increasing equity in athletics in schools, it has also been used as a legal basis to address sexual harassment and sexual assault in educational settings. In 2011, the Office for Civil Rights within the Department of Education issued a *Dear Colleague* letter in which they clarified that "The sexual harassment of students, including sexual violence, interferes with students' right to receive an education free from discrimination . . ." (U.S. Department of Education, 2011). Sexual harassment of students is also prohibited under the Civil Rights Act of 1964, which protects students from discrimination based on their sex, race, color, and national origin. Section 504 of the Rehabilitation Act of 1973 and Title II of the Americans with Disabilities Act protect students who have a documented disability. Under these laws, children with disabilities have a right to a free, appropriate, and safe education. This includes the right to be protected against bullying on the basis of their disability. Some states have laws that explicitly address how educational systems should teach about issues of diversity. For example, the FAIR Education Act, which was passed in California in 2011, required schools to provide factual information about LGBT individuals and people with disabilities and prevents the adoption of discriminatory instruction materials (FAIR Education Act, n.d.).

Laws in the United States do not apply to all aspects of identity that may make a child a target for identity-based bullying. As of the writing of this book, there is not a federal law explicitly protecting students from harassment and bullying based on their sexual orientation, although some states do have laws that offer such protection. As of 2015, two federal laws (the Student Non-Discrimination Act and the Safe Schools Improvement Act) were pending. These laws would provide additional protection for students against bullying and harassment in schools, particularly addressing bullying on the basis of actual or perceived sexual orientation and gender identity. Students may be protected if they are targeted because they engage in gender-atypical behaviors (which would lead to protection based on sex).

In addition to laws in the U.S. that protect children from discrimination, regulations have been proposed that would protect children from bullying. The U.S. Department of Education and President Obama sponsored the first ever Bullying Prevention Summit in 2010 at the White House. The Obama administration also used the event to unveil a new campaign to prevent bullying (StopBullying.gov). Many responded to the summit with enthusiasm and saw this move as an important step in addressing and preventing bullying in a systematic manner. While having laws and policies about bullying is important, sometimes the focus on bullying has led schools to neglect their legal responsibilities regarding protecting students from discrimination. In fact, in response to a growing trend of school districts using anti-bullying programs that do not address identity, schools have been reminded of their legal responsibility to protect children against discrimination and harassment. In 2010, the U.S. Department of Education Office for Civil

Rights made a call for schools' anti-bullying programs to address identity directly. A *Dear Colleague* letter from the assistant secretary for Civil Rights clearly defines how schools should be addressing such issues. They clarify that some behaviors that schools categorize as bullying should also be considered forms of discrimination (Ali, 2010). Further, the letter warns schools that generic anti-bullying programs may be insufficient. ". . . by limiting its response to a specific application of its anti-bullying disciplinary policy, a school may fail to properly consider whether the student misconduct also results in discriminatory harassment" (Ali, 2010).

Laws in the United Kingdom

Educational policies within the United Kingdom explicitly label identity-based bullying and describe educators' responsibilities for prevention and response (Tippett, Houlston, & Smith, 2010). There are two areas of legal policy within the United Kingdom that apply to identity-based bullying and inform these policies. First, bullying that includes violence, repeated harassment, theft, or hate crimes are all illegal forms of behavior that schools are expected to report to police (Gov.UK, 2014). Second, bullying that reflects discrimination is illegal according to either the Equality Act 2010 (an antidiscrimination law applying to England, Wales, and Scotland) or a collection of antidiscrimination laws that apply in Northern Ireland (Equality Commission for Northern Ireland, 2015). The Equality Act 2010 was designed to be a streamlined law that brought together many existing laws that addressed antidiscrimination as well as introduce additional needed protections. Interested readers are encouraged to read the entire law through the Equality and Human Rights Commission (EHRC) (Equality and Human Rights Commission, 2014). The EHRC and OFSTED provide guidance to schools in the United Kingdom about how to appropriately apply antidiscrimination law. The law protects children from discrimination on the basis of their sex, sexual orientation, religion, race, disability, and gender reassignment. The OFSTED provides schools with guidance to recognize identity-based bullying and to respond to the behavior as both a violation of schools' anti-bullying policies as well as an infraction against antidiscrimination laws.

CLIMATE OF SCHOOLS

Understanding the laws and government policies pertaining to identity-based bullying is an important step in examining how and why it persists. However, even when anti-bullying laws exist and schools do their best to follow them, sometimes the actual climate of the school may reflect different values than those captured by such documents. A school's climate and culture can provide clues about whether and how identity-based bullying may manifest.

Stover (2005) argues that an important distinction should be made between a school's culture and climate. The school climate consists of the *feel* of a place, the social atmosphere of a school that includes the unwritten rules of the school as well as the interactions that occur between and among students, teachers, and administrators (Hinduja & Patchin, 2012). The climate reflects how students and staff feel about their school and includes areas that may be susceptible to change. The culture of a school includes the underlying values and beliefs held by those within the school and may be harder to change than the climate. While most work on bullying focuses on the climate (what is happening within a particular school), a social justice perspective suggests that it is essential to understand the underlying culture influencing the community members within a school. This culture can impact the hidden curriculum of the school—the lessons taught that are not openly intended but often convey the values of the educators (Meighan & Harber, 2007). Educational institutions may explicitly endorse multicultural initiatives; but if they do not assess what is being conveyed within the hidden curriculum, such plans will lack energy and effectiveness (Jay, 2003). Without attending to the hidden curriculum in schools, anti-bullying interventions may create very specific and short-term changes (i.e., teachers increasing their response to name calling for a semester following an in-service about verbal bullying) but may be less likely spur on lasting and widespread change.

Understanding how the school environment contributes to individual students' experiences of victimization is essential. For example, students' perceptions of their schools' policies about sexual orientation and whether or not there are LGBT friendly programs predicts the prevalence and tolerance of identity-based bullying in their schools. In one study, students who reported that their school had active programs (such as Gay-Straight Alliances) also reported lower levels of victimization than students in schools were these programs did not exist (Chesir-Teran & Hughes, 2009). Interestingly, in this study, the presence of these programs was more impactful on student perceptions of victimization than were antidiscrimination policies. These findings are complex to understand, because schools that have antidiscrimination policies are more likely to also have supportive programming. However, this study indicates that while policies do matter, antidiscrimination programming may be more impactful than written policies alone.

CONCLUSION

Although some educational policies and laws may create barriers to addressing identity-based bullying within schools, mental health professionals and educators should be knowledgeable about the legal landscape and may be able to find ways to use educational law to support social justice work. For example, Goodenow, Szalacha, and Westheimer (2006) noted that NCLB mandated schools be safe learning environments for all individuals. So while this law in practice often led to diminished resources for diversity programs, savvy individuals could actually utilize it to make a case for increased programming to deter identity-based bullying. Educators and scholars can also advocate for new laws and policies and work to change educational structures so that they become spaces that promote equity and justice.

REFERENCES

Ali, R. (2010, October 26). [Dear Colleague Letter]. U.S. Department of Education Office of the Assistant Secretary. Retrieved from http://www2.ed.gov/about/offices/list/ocr/letters/colleague-201010.html

Au, W., Bigelow, B., & Karp, S. (2007). Introduction: Creating classrooms for equity and social justice. *Rethining Our Classrooms, 1,* x–xi.

Brinkman, B. G., & Manning, L. (2015). Children's intended responses to gender-based bullying as targets and bystanders. Manuscript under review.

Burgess, S., Briggs, A., McConnell, B., & Slater, H. (2006). *School choice in England: Background facts* (CMPO Working Paper No. 06/159). Bristol, England: Centre for Market and Public Organisation.

Center for Public Education. (n.d.). *The role of school boards.* Retrieved from http://www.centerforpubliceducation.org/You-May-Also-Be-Interested-In-landing-page-level/Audience-The-Public-YMABI/The-Role-of-School-Boards

Chesir-Teran, D., & Hughes, D. (2009). Heterosexism in high school and victimization among lesbian, gay, bisexual and questioning youth. *Journal of Youth and Adolescence, 38,* 963–975. doi: 10.1007/s10964-008-9364-x

Equality Commission for Northern Ireland. (2015). *Equality Commission for Northern Ireland.* Retrieved from http://www.equalityni.org/Delivering-Equality

Equality and Human Rights Commission. (2014, December 16). *What is the equality act?* Retrieved from http://www.equalityhumanrights.com/legal-and-policy/key-legislatures/equality-act-2010/what-is-the-equality-act

FAIR Education Act. (n.d.). *About FAIR.* Retrieved from http://www.faireducationact.com/about-fair/

Farnen, R. F. (2007). Class matters: Inequality, SES, education and childhood in the USA and Canada today. *Policy Futures in Education, 5,* 278–302.

Goodenow, C., Szalacha, L., & Westheimer, K. (2006). School support groups, other school factors, and the safety of sexual minority adolescents. *Psychology in the Schools, 43,* 573–589. doi: 10.1002/pits.20173

Gov.UK. (2014, November 12). *Bullying at school.* Retrieved from https://www.gov.uk/bullying-at-school/the-law

Green, J. E. (2001). *Education in the United Kingdom and Ireland (Studies in education).* Bloomington, IN: Phi Delta Kappa International.

Hinduja, S., & Patchin, J. W. (2012). *School climate 2.0: Preventing cyberbullying and sexting one classroom at a time.* Thousand Oaks, CA: Corwin.

Hoxby, C. M. (2002). *School choice and school productivity (or could school choice be a tide that lifts all boats?)* (NBER Working Paper No. 8873). Cambridge, MA: National Bureau of Economic Research.

Jay, M. (2003). Critical race theory, multicultural education, and the hidden curriculum of hegemony. *Multicultural Perspectives, 5,* 3–9.

Jennings, J., & Rentner, D. S. (2006, October). Ten big effects of the No Child Left Behind Act on public schools. *Phi Delta Kappan.* Retrieved from http://www.cep-dc.org/displayDocument.cfm?DocumentID=263

Kellner, D., & Share, J. (2005). Toward critical media literacy: Core concepts, debates, organizations and policy. *Discourse: Studies in the Cultural Politics of Education, 26*, 369–386.

Lubienski, C., Gulosino, C., & Weitzel, P. (2009). School choice and competitive incentives: Mapping the distribution of educational opportunities across local education markets. *American Journal of Education, 115*, 601–647.

Marley, D. (2008, May 30). Mind the performance gaps. Final part: The combined impact of gender, race, and class. *Times Educational Supplement*. Retrieved from http://www.tes.co.uk/article.aspx?storycode=2628662

Meighan, R., & Harber, C. (2007). *A sociology of educating* (5th ed.). New York, NY: Continuum International Publishing Group.

Murphy, T. (2014, September/October). Inside the mammoth backlash to common core: How a bipartisan education reform effort became the biggest conservative boogeyman since Obamacare. *Mother Jones*. Retrieved from http://www.motherjones.com/politics/2014/09/common-core-education-reform-backlash-obamacare

Ohio History Connection. (2013, July 11). *Indianola Junior High School*. Retrieved March 16, 2015, from http://www.ohiohistorycentral.org/w/Indianola_Junior_High_School?rec=2691

Porter, A., McMaken, J., Hwang, J., & Yang, R. (2011). Common core standards: The new U.S. intended curriculum. *Educational Researcher, 40*, 103–116. doi: 10.3102/0013189X11405038

Ravitch, D. (2010). *The death and life of the great American school system: How testing and choice are undermining education*. New York, NY: Basic Books.

Rury, J. L. (2012). *Education and social change: Contours in the history of American schooling* (4th ed.). New York, NY: Routledge.

Smith, E. (2012). *Key issues in education and social justice*. Thousand Oaks, CA: SAGE.

Stover, D. (2005). Climate and culture: Why your board should pay attention to the attitudes of students and staff. *American School Board Journal, 12*, 192.

Taylor, C. (2009). Choice, competition, and segregation in a United Kingdom urban education market. *American Journal of Education, 115*, 549–568.

Tippett, N., Houlston, C., & Smith, P. K. (2010). *Prevention and response to identity-based bullying among local authorities in England, Scotland, and Wales* (Research report 64). London, England: Equality and Human Rights Commission.

U.S. Department of Education. (2011, April 4) "Dear Colleague letter". Retrieved from http://www2.ed.gov/about/offices/list/ocr/letters/colleague-201104.html

Weber, K. (2010). *Waiting for Superman: How we can save America's failing public schools*. New York, NY: Public Affairs.

6 Challenges and Barriers to Addressing Identity-Based Bullying

I believe educators, scholars, and mental health professionals can find ways to effectively address identity-based bullying, but I do not intend to imply that the solutions will be easy. Identity-based bullying results from a complex interplay of factors; therefore, preventing and effectively responding to it is complicated and challenging. However, working on this issue can also be rewarding and have positive ripple effects—improving not only solitary schools but changing the larger culture by raising children to treat all people with dignity and respect, to celebrate differences, and to be compassionate citizens invested in equality.

There will be many challenges and barriers facing those individuals who are willing to confront identity-based bullying and the structures that reinforce it. Acknowledging possible struggles and making a plan to overcome them increases the likelihood of creating effective and sustainable changes. That is why this chapter precedes the recommendations. While this chapter is not all-inclusive (there are likely barriers I cannot foresee and ones I do not have space to address), I do outline some of the most common challenges facing those interested in tackling identity-based bullying and provide ideas about how to handle these barriers. In particular, I discuss challenges related to insufficient resources, anti-bullying policies and their implementation, difficulties engaging students, and barriers facing adult bystanders. I draw upon my own experiences working with schools and the barriers I have encountered while also integrating the lessons learned by others doing similar work.

RESOURCES

I start this chapter with resources because in some ways these are the most obvious and direct challenges to discuss. However, the apparently simplistic nature of these barriers makes them no less important and no easier to overcome. There are multiple types of challenges that could fall under the category of *resources* but I am going to discuss three significant ones: time, money, and expertise. There are certainly ways in which these three resources intersect, compounding their difficulty, but I will attempt to discuss them individually.

Time

The first important resource that may present challenges for those interested in eradicating identity-based bullying is time. As discussed in Chapter 5, school reforms that emphasized high-stakes testing (such as the No Child Left Behind policy in the U.S.) impacted the way schools allocated instructional time. Many critics argued that NCLB created pressure in schools to change their curriculum to focus more on improving test scores (Walker, 2014). In fact, numerous schools in the USA reported they did increase the amount of instructional time that was devoted to math and the language arts, sometimes at the expense of noninstructional time (like recess) and other subjects (such as the arts, social sciences, and music) (Cawelti, 2006; Powell, Higgins, Aram, & Freed, 2009). Although there are more studies on the impact of high-stakes testing on curriculum in the U.S. than the U.K., some research suggests that similar educational policies have had a narrowing effect on the curriculum of British schools (Berliner, 2011; Reay & Wiliam, 1999). Schools that cut or reduced subjects that were long considered core to the curriculum (such as physical education or social sciences) probably also cut out time for programming that could be considered "extra" curricular. This may have included diversity programming taking place on a school-wide level or social justice education that occurs in smaller doses within the classroom. In fact, one study found that during the 2008 presidential election in the United States, some government teachers were reluctant to discuss current political events (although they expressed a desire to do so), because they were afraid it may detract from material that was designed to help students do well on the end-of-year test (Journell, 2010). This finding suggests that teachers may forego opportunities to discuss ways that diversity impacts real world issues (such as the influence of race in a presidential election) because of pressures resulting from high-stakes testing.

The No Child Left Behind Act has not been reauthorized by Congress (as of the writing of this book), and many states have received waivers from the law and have instead set their own goals for achievement targets (Klein, 2014). As a result, schools are not under the same amount of pressure to adapt their curriculum in order to comply with NCLB; however, the restructuring that took place in response to this policy will likely continue unless there is new pressure to change. The decision about how schools want to spend their time may be a reflection of what the school values. Convincing a school that addressing identity-based bullying is an important enough topic to warrant the use of limited time may be the first challenge that a scholar or educator faces.

One way to address this challenge is for educators to find ways to integrate material about social issues and diversity with the required material that a school already offers. For example, teachers may be expected to dedicate a set amount of time to practice reading comprehension but might have flexibility about what students read. They could use that as an opportunity to introduce students to topics connected to social justice, including readings to help them embrace differences and information that supports them in becoming engaged global citizens. Students can read vignettes outlining experiences of identity-based bullying and brainstorm ways to respond with teachers and peers. They might also read stories that expand their exposure to people with a diversity of backgrounds in regard to ethnicity, social class, sexual orientation, religion, etc. Science and math teachers can be intentional about teaching students about a diverse group of scientists and mathematicians, being sure to teach students about females in STEM fields, and to highlight accomplishments of people of color and nonheterosexual scientists. Teachers can draw from resources such as the Smithsonian's list of female scientists (Zielinski, 2011) to ensure that all students in the classroom learn about role models who share their gender identity. Teachers may find that they can draw on projects integrating technology into the classroom to expand what students learn and present an equitable approach to the curriculum. For example, history teachers can utilize the Women on the Map project developed by the SPARK movement and hosted on Google's phone app *Field Trip* (Women on the Map, n.d.). The app will create an alert whenever the phone is approaching a landmark connected to one of over 100 women who have been profiled for the project.

Financial Considerations

The second challenge to effectively implementing programming to deter identity-based bullying is often directly related to time, and it involves financial resources. Most U.S. states cut their budgets for funding to K–12 school districts during the 2007–2009 recession. Many of those budget cuts have continued, with 35 states spending less in the 2013–2014 school year than they did before the recession (Leachman & Mai, 2014). In the U.K. (in England especially), growing populations in primary schools are resulting in budget gaps as costs are rising faster than funding is increasing (Coughlan, 2014). As a result, schools are forced to make tough financial decisions and rarely have extra revenue to dedicate to new programming.

When a school or school district engages in a prepackaged anti-bullying program, many teachers and administrators assume that the "bullying problem" has found a solution. They may be reluctant to invest more money in a new program, even if the programming they use has limitations. I have experienced this firsthand in my consultation work with schools. While reaching out to schools about social justice programming, many responded that they were not interested because they already had an anti-bullying program in place. While some of these programs may have fully addressed identity-based bullying, I suspect that most did not. In fact, during meetings with school officials, some teachers at these schools told me that they had concerns that their anti-bullying programming did not adequately attend to issues related to social identity. Unfortunately, at that point, many resources (in time and money) had already been devoted to the existing program, and school administrators were reluctant to consider additional programming.

There are ways to make programming about identity-based bullying cost-effective. School officials may elect to write grant proposals to receive funding from outside sources to help support such efforts. Collaborations between K–12 schools and colleges/universities may be especially helpful in this regard, as many university professors have expertise in applying for and overseeing grants. As I will discuss extensively in Chapter 7 (recommendations), I encourage schools to develop and utilize programming that best fits their needs. This may require some investment initially in the form of a needs assessment of the school and time spent researching potential programs; however, this approach can decrease waste of time and money in the long run.

Expertise

Limitations in both time and money can also impact the third possible challenge related to resources—expertise. Teachers, school officials, and administrators often lack the necessary training to recognize and effectively address identity-based bullying. Later in this chapter, I discuss the various interpersonal and intrapersonal dynamics within schools that may impact school officials' responses to identity-based bullying. But it is important to note that even if teachers address their own individual psychological barriers and schools manage the interpersonal dynamics that could block effective identity-based bullying prevention, teachers still need the training and expertise to put good intentions into effective action.

Truly eradicating identity-based bullying in schools will require ensuring that teachers receive comprehensive training regarding identity-based bullying, laws about discrimination and harassment, and recommendations about how to respond effectively. Within the U.K., teachers routinely receive training about diversity, as it is part of the national curriculum. However, one report that reviewed the implementation of the diversity curriculum in British schools suggests that teachers may be lacking in some knowledge about diversity and questioned the effectiveness of teacher training in this area (Maylor & Read, 2007). Within the United States, teacher preparation requirements are complicated by the fact that most are set by individual states and thus can vary widely nationwide. However, a 2008 report by the Civil Rights Project in collaboration with the Southern Poverty Law Center attempted to examine the preparation of teachers to address diversity issues in the classroom by surveying over 1,000 educators throughout the U.S. (Frankenberg & Siegel-Hawley, 2008). They found that most teachers were not prepared to use techniques that encouraged racially diverse groups and more than one-third had little or no training in supporting students who were English language learners. A more promising trend indicated that newer teachers reported having received more training in diversity issues, although many were critical of the tools they would have to implement this training in the classroom.

Regardless of the training that teachers (and other school personnel such as counselors and administrators) receive during their own undergraduate and graduate education, schools need to develop and support continued expertise of their staff on an ongoing basis. As I have explored in numerous ways throughout this text, it is apparent that the various dynamics influencing identity-based bullying in schools shift over time. The social issues of most pressing concern (and those that are most discussed) will also change over time. Schools can offer workshops and in-service training opportunities for current teachers, counselors, and administrators to support ongoing education about identity-based bullying.

IMPACT OF ANTI-BULLYING POLICIES

Despite limitations in resources (particularly related to time and money), many schools in the U.S. and the U.K. do implement some form of anti-bullying program—either because they believe it is important or because they have been pressured by outside forces to do so. Unfortunately, some of the efforts (including policies and programs) that have been implemented may actually create challenges to effectively counter identity-based bullying from a social justice perspective. Schools that already have an anti-bullying program and/or policies in place may be reluctant to spend the time and energy to assess their approach to ensure that it effectively addresses identity-based bullying. Further, the ways in which bullying is defined and policies designed to punish bullies can create barriers to effectively address identity-based bullying from a social justice perspective. These problems may be more acute in the U.S. than the U.K. where identity-based bullying has been more clearly defined. The Equality and Human Rights Commission within the United Kingdom has provided numerous resources for schools in England, Scotland, and Wales outlining the steps they should take to prevent and respond to identity-based bullying (Tippett, Houlston, & Smith, 2010). In addition to addressing the barriers listed below, scholars and educators within the United States may benefit from learning more about the approach taken within the United Kingdom.

Scholars have argued that anti-bullying programs/campaigns being used in the U.S. may be effective at preventing some forms of bullying but most do not account for identity and prejudice-related bullying (Bickmore, 2011; Richardson & Miles, 2008). The Olweus Bullying Prevention Program is perhaps the most commonly utilized and cited model for anti-bullying programming in schools. Findings suggest that the forms of bullying targeted by the program decreases as much as 50% after participation in the program (Limber, 2004). The goals of the curriculum include reducing existing bullying problems, preventing future problems, and improving peer relationships (Olweus, 1991). Other anti-bullying programs that utilize similar theoretical frameworks have also been implemented within the United States, with some promising findings regarding their ability to decrease bullying incidents (Jenson, Dieterich, Brisson, Bender, & Powell, 2010). Schools may implement one of these programs because of the research demonstrating their effectiveness; however, these types of programs may not be effective at addressing identity-based bullying. Most do not take into consideration the sociocultural factors that play into the power-control scenarios in bullying (Swearer, Espelage, Vaillancourt, & Hymel, 2010) and discussions of the intersection of bullying and social identity are often neglected. These programs often emphasize individual characteristics without recognizing the larger social context in which bullying behaviors occur, including the factors that contribute to identity-based bullying.

Definitions of Bullying

Whether or not a school has an anti-bullying policy in place, the traditional definitions of bullying can at times be a hindrance to individuals interested in addressing identity-based bullying. Much of Chapter 1 of this book is devoted to developing a definition of identity-based bullying and discussing the complications of such a definition. However, it is worth revisiting this discussion here, as definitions impact the way adults address incidents in school. In fact, one of the biggest challenges to effectively addressing identity-based bullying may be that school administrators are not sure what it is. Many traditional definitions of bullying do not address social identity and do not define identity-based bullying. Policies and programs designed to address bullying may be vague about prejudice-related bullying. This vagueness can leave teachers and other school officials unclear about whether or how to address these specific behaviors.

In addition to lack of clarity about the intersection of bullying and discrimination, traditional conceptualizations of bullying can also have other implications for the ways educators think about the problem of identity-based bullying. For example, bullying is often defined as consisting of repetitive behaviors. This aspect of the definition may be important in clarifying the difference between a onetime conflict among students and bullying. However, the practical applications of this definition, especially as it concerns identity-based bullying, can pose challenges. What happens if an educator only hears a comment once? Does this constitute bullying? What if a student is targeted with identity-based bullying in such a way that most of the behavior occurs in settings where adults are not present? The emphasis on repetitive behaviors can also be problematic because of the implication that some behaviors are only unacceptable if they are repeated. What message does it send to students if a teacher ignores one student calling another student a *fag*, or sexually harassing a female, or using a racist epithet all because these incidents only occurred once? Rather than focusing on the frequency with which one specific student says something to another specific student, effectively addressing identity-based bullying requires an approach that considers the entire culture of the school. While being a target of one of these comments just once likely does not do long-term damage to a student, hearing them repeatedly (even if by different perpetrators) or worrying about hearing them can certainly be harmful. Although I do not pose that there is any easy answer to this question, I think it is important to consider the underlying goal of eradicating identity-based bullying. If a school seeks to create an environment that fosters respect, celebrates diversity, and encourages development of students into world citizens, focusing only on repetitive behaviors may not be sufficient.

Zero Tolerance Policies

Other policies that some schools have adopted in their quest to demonstrate that they are handling bullying may also become a hindrance to effectively detecting, preventing, and intervening in cases of identity-based bullying. Some schools in the U.S. have implemented zero tolerance policies, designed to punish any student engaging in bullying. Many scholars have argued that these policies are flawed and are ineffective at decreasing bullying (Brown, Chesney-Lind, & Stein, 2007; Klein, 2012; Stein, 2001). These policies often result in the punishment of children who are repeatedly victimized by others and finally lash out in frustration. For example, girls in schools with zero tolerance policies may find themselves being penalized for defending themselves against bullying and harassment (Crenshaw, Ocen, & Nanda, 2015), compounding their negative experiences. In some cases, students and even teachers may be less likely to report bullying when zero tolerance policies are in place, because they do not want a child to experience severe punishment, like being expelled from the school (Mulvey & Cauffman, 2001). Research on zero tolerance policies indicates that the policies are disproportionately applied to students of color, particularly to Black children, often resulting in the suspension or expulsion of students (Ayers, Dohm, & Ayers, 2001). In the 2011–2012 school year, Black female students were suspended six times more often than White females, and Black males were suspended three times more often than White male students (Crenshaw et al., 2015). These policies may not only be ineffective at deterring identity-based bullying, but may in fact contribute to an inequitable school climate where children learn that it is "acceptable" to treat people differently based on their racial/ethnic identity.

ENGAGING STUDENTS

Addressing identity-based bullying from a social justice perspective includes considering the context of the school and the interactions of the children or adolescents within it. Schools in the U.S. and U.K. rarely function as democracies, and students typically have little say in the policies and procedures of the school (Hemming, 1980). However, educators can shift their thinking about the potential for students to play a proactive role in shaping the school environment and deterring identity-based bullying. Implementing a systems-wide approach to identity-based bullying utilizing a social justice perspective requires engaging students in a meaningful way.

There are a number of reasons that students may resist participating in anti-bullying or social justice programming. Even if students see the potential importance of social issues, they may feel that other concerns have higher priority. Students who are dealing with significant stressors in their lives (living with a sick relative, witnessing violence in their homes, or experiencing financial instability) may not feel that they have the emotional resources or interest to invest in a school's attempt to discuss social issues. Second, students may not want to address identity-based bullying if they are focusing on their reputation or social life. Ironically, students who may benefit the most from anti-bullying work may be the most resistant to discussions about social identities. Those students who are most anxious about their own social identity and whether or not they "measure up" (in terms of conformity to gender norms, fitting into social-class expectations, etc.) may be reluctant to talk about these issues for fear of drawing attention to themselves. As discussed in Chapter 3, some children who are trying to conform may engage in identity-based bullying against others as a means of diverting attention away from themselves. Whatever the reason, some students may avoid discussions regarding social justice and identity-based bullying, they may minimize or be dismissive of programming in this area, or they may become overtly resistant (and perhaps even disrespectful) to manage their own anxiety about the topics.

Educators may not always be aware of the dynamics within a student's life and may be tempted to interpret any resistance to anti-bullying programming as a sign of disrespect. Teachers may become especially frustrated with these students who are labeled as *bullies* or *troublemakers*. While teachers may not always know the causes of a student's lack of engagement, it may be helpful for facilitators of identity-based bullying to consider resistance as a potential indicator that a child needs more compassion. Rather than being reactive to students' responses, if facilitators can attempt to observe students with an awareness of these possibilities, they may understand students' reactions in a new way. Educators may learn valuable information about students by noticing when they have strong reactions to the material. They can make note of students who seem especially reluctant to engage in the material and consider whether it will be helpful to attend to that student individually. Educators and school counselors should avoid labeling children and consider that each student is potentially responding to multiple dynamics in his or her own life. Facilitators can set the expectation that respect is necessary without becoming so frustrated with a particular student that they respond dismissively or with contempt or disdain. Reaching the most challenging students may turn out to be the most influential in creating lasting change in the school environment.

It may also be challenging to present the material in a way that encourages buy-in of all students. Scholars, educators, mental health professionals, and advocates who have done social justice work with heterogeneous populations of any age have likely struggled with this challenge—how do you reach an audience with a range of experiences? Students who experience or who witness discrimination and harassment based on aspects of social identity may be especially likely to dismiss approaches that they see as being unrealistic or out of touch. They may also feel further marginalized by interventions that are designed to raise the awareness of their peers who are in a majority group. For example, a common educational tool used to teach students about diversity includes a *privilege walk* where students start on one horizontal line and take steps forward or backward during the activity depending upon their experiences of privilege. Students who were previously unaware of their privilege may report that they find this activity illuminating. However, students who end up at the back of the room may feel singled out or as though their life experiences are used as a teaching tool for others in the classroom.

Students may also differ in their awareness of various forms of discrimination and identity-based bullying depending upon their own identity. Children who are unaware of others' experiences of discrimination may minimize the need for conversations about equity. Some of these students may not even be aware of the ways identity can impact people's lived experiences. One study found that three-fourths of youth were aware of gender bias, but only approximately half of their participants were aware of ethnic bias (Brown, Alabi, Huynh, & Masten, 2011). European American/White children in the study were much less likely to recognize ethnic bias than were children of color. Students were also more likely to notice when another member of their group experienced discrimination than when they were the target themselves. Access to privileges as a White person may make it less likely for a child to realize the role race/ethnicity plays in society (McDermott & Samson, 2005).

Even when children/adolescents are educated about social identities, some may be reluctant to give up privilege related to this identity. Identity-based bullying is an expression of power dynamics within hierarchical structures—students who have access to resources by excluding and mistreating others may not want those power dynamics to shift. While it may be challenging to do so, engaging students in the work is crucial. Addressing identity-based bullying will be most effective if students are motivated and if adults recognize that children may have multiple emotional reactions to the work that need to be attended to.

ADULTS AS BYSTANDERS

Approaching identity-based bullying within schools utilizing a social justice perspective involves addressing a number of dynamics among adults within the school system. One way to better understand the interpersonal and intrapersonal dynamics influencing adults is to conceptualize them as potential bystanders during incidents of bullying (Anderson, 2011).

Confronting Prejudiced Responses Model

The Confronting Prejudiced Responses Model (CPR) (Ashburn-Nardo, Morris, & Goodwin, 2008) is commonly used to examine the decision-making process that bystanders engage in as they decide whether or not to intervene when they witness discrimination. Here I apply this model to explore the various factors that may influence how adult educators (teachers, administrators, counselors, etc.) respond to identity-based bullying and to highlight the possible barriers to intervention. The CPR model proposes bystanders undergo a five-step decision-making process when faced with prejudicial interactions. In order to take action, a bystander must interpret an event as discrimination, decide that it is potentially harmful to the target, take responsibility for intervening, consider the possible responses, and then take action. At each of these steps, adult educators may weigh various factors (and be influenced subconsciously by various factors) to determine whether they will intervene. Each of these steps may present barriers that can decrease the likelihood of educators responding proactively to identity-based bullying.

Step 1: An Adult Must Know that the Event is Happening and Must be Able to Appropriately Label it as Identity-Based Bullying

While this seems an obvious step, there are many potential barriers even at this first stage. Identity-based bullying might be subtle and/or occur in spaces where teachers are not present to see it (bathroom, locker room, etc.) (Anderson, 2011). Students may avoid telling adults about bullying that occurs in these hidden spaces if teachers are seen as bullies, if students think they will not be believed, or if they think the teacher will not intervene (Strauss, 2012). Even if teachers know that a behavior is happening, they must also be able to identify it as identity-based bullying. As discussed previously, most traditional definitions of bullying do not account for identity-based bullying, leaving adult educators uncertain how to label specific behaviors. While I have tried to provide a useful definition within this book, the application to the real world is certainly murkier. However, schools can face this first challenge head-on by including identity-based bullying in their anti-bullying policies, by discussing how teachers should respond when they witness an (apparently) one-time interaction and encouraging conversation among educators about how to respond when incidents appear to be vague or the situation is unclear.

Step 2: An Adult Must Determine that the Behavior is Potentially Harmful

Teachers, administrators, school counselors, or other adults have to determine that a behavior is potentially harmful to the target in order to be motivated to intervene. One qualitative study about bullying found that teachers' definition of and response to incidents was impacted by whether they thought an event was serious and if they felt the child was congruent with their assumptions about victims (Mishna, Scarcello, Pepler, & Wiener, 2005). Many teachers will identify a behavior as bullying and be concerned about the impact it could have on students. However, sometimes educators will label an event as bullying but not intervene because they either 1) minimize the impact of identity-based bullying or 2) actually condone the bullying.

Some adult educators accept identity-based bullying as being normative and inevitable and as such not a reason for concern. While most teachers believe that bullying that becomes physically violent is harmful, several minimize the negative impact of teasing or exclusion. Adults may think kids should learn to handle situations by themselves (Strauss, 2012) and that learning to ignore being teased or excluded is a way to "toughen up" for the real world. If teachers endorse a decontextualized model of bullying, they may not "see" identity-based bullying or harassment that is taking place in their classrooms. For example, many teachers report that they think sexual harassment and other forms of gender-based bullying are normal (Strauss, 2012). Teachers' own past and current experiences with bullying and harassment may also influence the extent to which they feel it is necessary to address identity-based bullying. Some may neglect to address bullying if they see this behavior as a legitimate form of socialization (Klein, 2012).

Unfortunately, in some extreme cases, identity-based bullying and harassment go unaddressed by school personnel because the educators themselves sanction the mistreatment. Teachers' own values and beliefs can reinforce oppression and patriarchal hierarchies (Strauss, 2012). Some teachers have internalized their own stereotypes about various groups and thus might think that mistreatment of a child is valid. This may be the case when aspects of social identities are the center of larger social controversies. For example, within the U.S., many Arab and Muslim children have experienced bullying related to Islamophobia. Numerous reports indicate that teachers often ignore the bullying and/or schools neglect to punish perpetrators (Holcomb, 2011). In some cases, teachers actually engage in the bullying behavior themselves (Sacirbey, 2011).

In order for adult educators to be proactive bystanders when students are engaging in identity-based bullying, they must see the harm that such behavior can cause. Educators and school personnel should become familiar with research demonstrating the harmful effects of identity-based bullying, come to terms with their own past experiences with bullying, and participate in activities to challenge their own internalized stereotypes.

Step 3: Adults Have to Take Responsibility for Intervening

Once adults have labeled identity-based bullying and decided that it is problematic, they must then determine that it is their responsibility to intervene. One area in which many adults within school systems struggle to assess their responsibility for taking action is in regard to cyberbullying. Although in this book I have focused on forms of bullying that take place within schools and through in-person encounters, it is essential to acknowledge that technology has created enormous challenges for addressing identity-based bullying. Students may engage in identity-based bullying by posting hurtful comments or photos on social media. Students may also call, text, or instant message each other both during school and outside of school. Many schools struggle with defining the boundaries of their responsibility for addressing this behavior. They worry about overstepping legal boundaries (*can* they intervene in events that happen out of school time and off school grounds) while also wanting to promote consistent messages about respectful behavior. Many teachers may feel stuck—is it their job to intervene if a student texts something during school hours? What if something happens on social media over the weekend but students talk about it in class on Monday? It is important for educators to consult with their school administrators to ensure they are in line with policies and laws that are rapidly changing in response to cyberbullying in particular. Educators can turn to resources about cyberbullying to gain more information and ideas about how to effectively respond (see Hinduja & Patchin, 2009, 2012 for more information).

It is important for educators to understand the extent of their legal responsibilities to address identity-based bullying and how it may differ from their legal responsibilities regarding other forms of bullying. Readers interested in guidelines within the U.S. may refer to Strauss's (2012) book *Sexual Harassment and Bullying: A Guide to Keeping Kids Safe and Holding Schools Accountable*, among other resources. She outlines how the Office of Civil Rights (OCR) and the federal courts are responsible for enforcing laws and determining a school's liability in discrimination cases (Strauss, 2012). Educators can also turn to the OCR, which provides assistance to school districts about how to prevent and stop sexual harassment and discrimination. In the United Kingdom, there may be less confusion about educators' legal responsibilities to address identity-based bullying, as it has been more fully integrated into legal definitions of bullying and educational policies. Individuals seeking additional resources can turn to the Equality and Human Rights Commission (who published the 2010 report *Prevention and Response to Identity-Based Bullying Among Local Authorities in England, Scotland and Wales*) or the RespectMe program in Scotland.

Educators' uncertainty about whether they have a legal responsibility to respond can be problematic if they become paralyzed by their indecision. One way to tackle this challenge is to step back and remember the larger goal of deterring identity-based bullying. If an educator is focused on creating a safe and equitable environment and supporting the development of students who value diversity and equality, these moments of uncertainty can be turned into moments of opportunity. In addition to addressing specific incidents that take place, educators can create learning opportunities in which they discuss the larger issues at hand. For example, if a teacher learns about an LGB student being bullied about his/her sexual orientation, the teacher may decide to examine how sexual orientation is being treated and discussed in that environment. Is heterosexist language used in the classroom (using terms like husband and wife instead of partner)? Do students regularly use derogatory terms such as *fag* or *queer*? The teacher can then take steps to address the entire class about issues related to sexual orientation by discussing inclusive language, ensuring that students learn about famous LGB individuals, and debunking stereotypes. Regardless of the type of identity-based bullying, educators can use this approach to work toward the larger goal of creating more just and inclusive schools. (See Chapter 7 for more recommendations about turning critical incidents into learning opportunities.)

Step 4: Adults Weigh the Potential Costs and Benefits of Action and Consider Their Options for Intervention

The next step is for adult educators to assess the possible methods of intervention to identity-based bullying and weigh the potential costs and benefits of each. Teachers may be hesitant to intervene during incidents of identity-based bullying if they do not think the school administration will support them or if they are concerned about potential backlash that could result from them speaking out. The values of the administration of a school are often conveyed in formal and informal ways. Written policies about how to define, prevent, and manage bullying convey messages to teachers and students about what is valued in the school (and what is not). Teachers who value diversity and social justice but work in a school where these values are not clearly defined by the administration may struggle when in deciding how to act when they witness identity-based bullying occurring. Teachers may not have as much control over their curriculum as they would like and may worry about losing their jobs if they step too far from the school's written goals or teach information that differs from the values of the headmaster or principal. While working on this project, I presented some of my research at the American Psychological Association convention and happened to be at a poster presentation next to a high school psychology teacher. When she learned about the work I was doing, she shared with me her experiences in her school. They had recently adopted new anti-bullying policies, but she found them to be somewhat confusing and vague. She was especially concerned about students in her school who identified as gay or who did not conform to stereotypical gender-role expression and who experienced regular bullying and harassment. Although teachers had been informed about the new anti-bullying policies, she did not feel confident that her administrators would support her in addressing the social identity issues. She wanted to more directly discuss issues of gender and sexual orientation but feared potential backlash from her administrators if she did.

Teachers' own social identities may also make it difficult for them to intervene, if they fear reprisals for doing so. In the U.S., LGBTQ educators and school counselors may be reluctant to speak out against homophobic bullying. Teachers who are gay and closeted may feel especially conflicted about how to manage homophobia in the classroom (Walters & Hayes, 1998). One recent study found that many LGBTQ teachers in the U.S. were hesitant to challenge homophobia because they were afraid that others would think they were gay, and they were fearful for their jobs (Bloom, 2013). Of the 350 teachers and principals who were interviewed, 75% said that they rarely or never heard another teacher challenge homophobia, and over half of the participants reported hearing teachers themselves make homophobic comments. As of the writing of this book, there is not a federal law within the United States that protects individuals from employment discrimination based on their sexual orientation. While some states have included LGBT individuals in their statutes of protection against employment discrimination, this is not uniform. In fact, as of 2013, 29 states had laws that allowed employers to fire someone simply because they thought the person might be gay (Brydum, 2013). Unfortunately, even having antidiscrimination laws that include sexual orientation may not be sufficient to protect teachers from harassment. One survey of LGBT teachers in the U.K. found that 66% experienced harassment or discrimination at work related to their sexual orientation or gender identity (Roberts, 2013).

Schools may also be reluctant to respond to identity-based bullying because of their concerns about reactions from parents. In general, parents may pressure teachers to ignore some problem behaviors that students engage in (Strauss, 2012). Parents may not be aware that their children are participating in bullying, and when informed by a school, some parents may be in denial (Duncan, 1999). In cultures with schools of choice, schools may also be worried about prospective parents' perceptions of the school. In one study, some British heads of schools indicated that they were worried that discussing bullying would make parents think they have a bullying problem

(Katz, Buchanan, & Bream, 2001). As a result, schools may prefer to suppress any discussion of identity-based bullying rather than face it directly.

Schools may also face pressure from parent groups who deem topics related to social identity as "too controversial" to discuss in schools. In Britain, there has been some resistance by parents who do not want their children to learn about Islam in schools. One such group created a Facebook page titled *British parents opposing Islamic indoctrination of British children.* In one incident, parents protested when students were told they were required to attend a university exhibit where they would learn about Islam (Taylor, 2013). After much outrage, parents were informed that they could withdraw their children from this activity. In the United States, similar battles have been waged between schools and parent groups regarding education about sexual orientation. Some parent groups have protested schools who attempted to include discussions of homophobia in their anti-bullying programs and policies. For example, in Alameda, California, one school discontinued its K–5 LGBT anti-bullying component following protests and a lawsuit from parents (Dacus, 2010). Pressures from parent groups may encourage schools to avoid discussions of diversity and to neglect to fully address identity-based bullying.

Step 5: Take Action

Finally, even if teachers have decided that intervention is warranted and they should do something, they may lack the skills to intervene effectively. Some will tell a perpetrator to "stop" their immediate behavior but do little else to address the situation (Anderson, 2011). However, if educators can at least get to the stage where they commit to take action, they will have navigated important steps to address the major challenges along the way. In Chapter 7, I provide recommendations about how to intervene effectively to deter identity-based bullying.

CONCLUSION

Eradicating identity-based bullying will not be an easy task. Scholars, educators, parents, and other professionals interested in creating more just schools will likely face many challenges along the way. Schools often worry about limited resources in terms of time and money, and individuals invested in addressing identity-based bullying may need to think creatively to provide effective programming within these limitations. Programs that work to actively engage students will likely see greater, longer-lasting results. Educators can elicit student involvement by recognizing the reasons they may be reluctant to participate in discussions about social identity and honoring the challenges and complexities students face. Finally, conceptualizing adult educators as potential bystanders to identity-based bullying may allow them to explore the common barriers to bystander intervention and tackle them one by one, hopefully increasing proactive responses. I believe that the vast majority of schools and administrators are genuinely interested in creating positive and supportive learning environments for all students. Recognizing the potential barriers and developing a plan to overcome them may make the difference in whether or not this work results in meaningful, lasting change.

REFERENCES

Anderson, S. (2011). *No more bystanders = no more bullies: Activating action in educational professionals*. Thousand Oaks, CA: Corwin.

Ashburn-Nardo, L., Morris, K. A., & Goodwin, S. A. (2008). The confronting prejudiced responses (CPR) model: Applying CPR in organizations. *Academy of Management Learning & Education, 7*, 332–342. doi: 10.5465/AMLE.2008.34251671

Ayers, W., Dohm, B., & Ayers, R. (Eds.). (2001). *Zero tolerance: Resisting the drive for punishment in our schools: A handbook for parents, students, educators and citizens*. New York, NY: The New Press.

Berliner, D. (2011). Rational responses to high stakes testing: The case of curriculum narrowing and the harm that follows. *Cambridge Journal of Education, 41*, 287–302. doi: 10.1080/0305764X.2011.607151

Bickmore, K. (2011). Policies and programming for safer schools: Are 'anti-bullying' approaches impeding education for peacebuilding? *Educational Policy, 25*(4), 648–687. doi: 10.1177/0895904810374849

Bloom, A. (2013, July 26). Gay teachers less likely to challenge homophobia. *TES connect*. Retrieved from https://www.tes.co.uk/article.aspx?storycode=6344655

Brown, C. S., Alabi, B. O., Huynh, V. W., & Masten, C. L. (2011). Ethnicity and gender in late childhood and early adolescence: Group identity and awareness of bias. *Developmental Psychology, 47*, 463–471.

Brown, L. M., Chesney-Lind, M., & Stein, N. (2007). Patriarchy matters: Toward a gendered theory of teen violence and victimization. *Violence Against Women, 13*, 1249–1273. doi: 10.1177/1077801207310430

Brydum, S. (2013, December 18). Meet the people fired for being LGBT in 2013. *The Advocate*. Retrieved from http://www.advocate.com/year-review/2013/12/18/meet-people-fired-being-lgbt-2013?page=full

Cawelti, G. (2006). The side effects of NCLB. *Educational Leadership, 64*(3), 64–68.

Coughlan, S. (2014). Primary school places budget squeeze. *BBC News*. Retrieved from http://www.bbc.com/news/education-28937664

Crenshaw, K. W., Ocen, P., & Nanda, J. (2015). *Black girls matter: Pushed out, overpoliced and underprotected*. A report from African American Policy Forum.

Dacus, B. (2010, May 20). *Alameda district discontinues K-5 LGBT curriculum; Parents dismiss opt-out suit* [Press release]. Retrieved from http://www.standardnewswire.com/news/789685233.html

Duncan, N. (1999). *Sexual bullying: Gender conflict and pupil culture in secondary schools*. London, England: Routledge.

Frankenberg, E. & Siegel-Hawley, G. (2008). Are teachers prepared for racially changing schools? Teachers describe their preparation, resources and practices for racially diverse schools. *Civil Rights Project*. Retrieved from: http://civilrightsproject.ucla.edu/research/k-12-education/integration-and-diversity/are-teachers-prepared-for-racially-changing-schools/frankenberg-are-teachers-prepared-racially.pdf

Hemming, J. (1980). *The betrayal of youth: Secondary education must be changed.* London, UK: Marion Boyars.

Hinduja, S., & Patchin, J. W. (2009). *Bullying beyond the schoolyard: Preventing and responding to cyberbullying.* Thousand Oaks, CA: Corwin Press.

Hinduja, S., & Patchin, J.W. (2012). *School climate 2.0: Preventing cyberbullying and sexting one classroom at a time.* Thousand Oaks, CA: Corwin.

Holcomb, S. (2011, December 3). Muslims in America: When bullying meets religion. *Muslim Matters.* Retrieved from http://muslimmatters.org/2011/12/13/muslims-in-america-when-bullying-meets-religion/

Jenson, J. M., Dieterich, W. A., Brisson, D., Bender, K. A., & Powell, A. (2010). Preventing childhood bullying: Findings and lessons from the Denver public schools trial. *Research on Social Work Practice, 20,* 509–517.

Journell, W. (2010). The influence of high-stakes testing on high school teachers' willingness to incorporate current political events into the curriculum. *The High School Journal, 93,* 111–125.

Katz, A., Buchanan, A., & Bream, V. (2001). *Bullying in Britain: Testimonies from teenagers.* London: Young Voice.

Klein, A. (2014, January 8). No child left behind turns 12 today. Now what? *Education Week.* Retrieved from http://blogs.edweek.org/edweek/campaign-k-12/2014/01/no_child_left_behind_turns_twe.html

Klein, J. (2012). *The bully society: School shootings and the crisis of bullying in America's schools.* New York, NY: New York University Press.

Leachman, M., & Mai, C. (2014, May 20). Most states funding schools less than before the recession. *Center on Budget and Policy Priorities.* Retrieved from http://www.cbpp.org/cms/?fa=view&id=4011#_ftn1

Limber, S.P. (2004). Implementation of the Olweus Bullying Prevention Program: Lessons learned from the field. In D. Espelage & S. Swearer (Eds.), *Bullying in American Schools: A Social-Ecological Perspective on Prevention and Intervention* (pp. 351–363). Mahwah, NJ: Lawrence Erlbaum.

Maylor, U., & Read, B. (2007). *Diversity and citizenship in the curriculum: Research review.* The Institute for Policy Studies in Education: London Metropolitan University.

McDermott, M., & Samson, F.L. (2005). White racial and ethnic identity in the United States. *Annual Review of Sociology, 31,* 245–261.

Mishna, F., Scarcello, I., Pepler, D., Wiener, J. (2005). Teachers' understanding of bullying. *Canadian Journal of Education, 28,* 718–738.

Mulvey, E.P., & Cauffman, E. (2001). The inherent limits of predicting school violence. *American Psychologist, 56,* 797–802. Retrieved from http://dx.doi.org/10.1037/0003-066X.56.10.797

Olweus, D. (1991). Bully/victim problems among schoolchildren: Basic facts and effects of a school-based intervention program. In D. J. Pepler & K. H. Rubin (Eds.), *The development and treatment of childhood aggression* (pp. 411–448). Hillsdale, NJ: Erlbaum.

Powell, D., Higgins, H.J., Aram, R., & Freed, A. (2009). Impact of No Child Left Behind on curriculum and instruction in rural schools. *The Rural Educator, 31,* 19–28.

Reay, D., & Wiliam, D. (1999). 'I'll be a nothing': Structure, agency and the construction of identity through assessment. *British Educational Research Journal, 25,* 343–354. doi: 10.1080/0141192990250305

Richardson, R., & Miles, B. (2008). *Racist incidents and bullying in schools.* Staffordshire, UK: Trentham Books Limited.

Roberts, S. (2013). Campaigners to research bullying against LGBT teachers. *Pink News.* Retrieved from http://www.pinknews.co.uk/2013/12/05/uk-campaigners-to-research-bullying-against-lgbt-teachers/

Sacirbey, O. (2011, September, 8). 9/11 Bullying: Muslim teens push back. *Huffington Post*. Retrieved from http://www.huffingtonpost.com/2011/09/07/bullying-muslim-teens-push-back_n_952947.html

Stein, N. (2001). Sexual harassment meets zero-tolerance: Life in K-12 schools. In W. Ayers, B. Dohrn, & R. Ayers (Eds.), *Zero tolerance: Resisting the drive for punishment: A handbook for parents, students, educators and citizens* (pp. 143–154). New York, NY: New Press.

Strauss, S. (2012). *Sexual harassment and bullying: A guide to keeping kids safe and holding schools accountable*. Plymouth, UK: Rowman & Littlefield Publishers.

Swearer, S. M., Espelage, D. L., Vaillancourt, T., & Hymel, S. (2010). What can be done about school bullying? Linking research to educational practice. *Educational Researcher, 39*, 38–47. doi: 10.3102/0013189X09357622

Taylor, R. (2013, November 22). Children of 8 are 'racist' if they miss Islam trip: School's threatening letter to parents is met with outrage. *The Daily Mail*. Retrieved from http://www.dailymail.co.uk/news/article-2511841/Children-8-racist-miss-Islam-trip-Schools-threatening-letter-parents-met-outrage.html

Tippett, N., Houlston, C., & Smith, P. K. (2010). *Prevention and response to identity-based bullying among local authorities in England, Scotland, and Wales* (Research report 64). London, England: Equality and Human Rights Commission.

Walker, T. (2014, September 2). The testing obsession and the disappearing curriculum. *NEA Today*. Retrieved from http://neatoday.org/2014/09/02/the-testing-obsession-and-the-disappearing-curriculum-2/

Walters, A. S., & Hayes, D. M. (1998). Homophobia within schools: Challenging the culturally sanctioned dismissal of gay students and colleagues. *Journal of Homosexuality, 35*, 1–23.

Women on the map. (n.d.). Retrieved from http://www.sparksummit.com/onthemap/

Zielinski, S. (2011, September 9). Ten historic female scientists you should know. *Smithsonian.com*. Retrieved from http://www.smithsonianmag.com/science-nature/ten-historic-female-scientists-you-should-know-84028788/?no-ist

7 Recommendations for Best Practices to Prevent and Respond to Identity-Based Bullying

The goal of this chapter is to provide recommendations for researchers, administrators, and educators for best practices to prevent and respond to identity-based bullying. I review research about specific programs currently utilized in schools within the U.S. and U.K., but overall I assert that a one-size-fits-all approach is not likely to be effective. Instead, I encourage stakeholders to build upon the lessons that others have learned, while also adapting specific programs in order to best fit the needs of their community. I provide a list of general recommendations, along with three case examples to demonstrate how to put these suggestions into action.

UTILIZING RESEARCH EVIDENCE

My first recommendation is for scholars and educators to be knowledgeable about the existing research evidence regarding the causes of and effective ways to intervene in identity-based bullying. This may seem like a daunting task, because it means not only reading the limited literature about identity-based or prejudice-related bullying, but also staying abreast of the literature about bullying, as well as the literature about discrimination against children.

The literature on anti-bullying programs is steadily growing, providing scholars and school officials interested in implementing programs with many resources for assessing what works and why. Overall, meta-analyses of anti-bullying programs have yielded mixed results regarding the efficacy of anti-bullying programs. A 2008 meta-analysis examining 16 studies (which included over 1,500 participants from the United States, Canada, and Europe) found that anti-bullying programs often resulted in changes in attitudes or beliefs about bullying but rarely changed behaviors (Merrell, Gueldner, Ross, & Isava, 2008). While the literature about bullying can be helpful, the challenge for schools is to not only understand what works but under what circumstances and for which students (Smith, Salmivalli, & Cowie, 2012). One meta-analysis sought to examine whether there were developmental differences in the effects of anti-bullying programs and found that programs were generally effective when administered in the seventh grade or below but had little to no impact when delivered in the eighth grade or beyond (Yeager, Fong, Lee, & Espelage, 2015).

Intergroup Contact and Other Prejudice Reduction Approaches

Not all anti-bullying programs integrate social identity into their framework, so schools should consider combining information that is available about anti-bullying programs with the literature about prejudice reduction among children. One meta-analysis of 81 research studies examining programs designed to either reduce prejudice among children or increase positive intergroup attitudes found overall beneficial impacts of such programs (Beelmann & Heinemann, 2014). Programs that had the strongest effects were those that encouraged empathy and perspective taking and utilized direct contact experiences, drawing upon intergroup contact theory. Intergroup contact theory suggests that having contact with members of a group different from one's own can decrease prejudice against that group (Pettigrew, 1998). There is a large body of literature examining how intergroup contact can lead to prejudice reduction (see Hewstone & Swart, 2011 and Pettigrew & Tropp, 2006 for reviews of the literature). Much of this research has been conducted with adults, but the findings may be adapted for work with older adolescents. For example, one study found that attending a peer panel of LGB students was a useful educational strategy in decreasing homophobia among college students (Nelson & Krieger, 1997).

There is also a growing body of work using intergroup contact activities to deter discrimination in children. For example, one study conducted in the United Kingdom found that programs using extended contact led to more positive attitudes among students toward children with disabilities and children from refugee groups (Cameron, Rutland, & Brown, 2007). Another study conducted in Britain found that children who had greater amounts of intergroup contact with immigrants had higher levels of cultural openness and endorsed less intergroup bias (Abbott & Cameron, 2014). These children also demonstrated more intentions to utilize assertive bystander interventions when reading vignettes about immigrant children being called names.

Findings from research studies about intergroup contact provide important information about the conditions under which it can help reduce prejudice. The quality of the interaction is important, as is the preparation of those who will engage in intergroup contact experiences. These are important caveats, and educators should not assume that simply forcing children to interact with members of other social groups will automatically dispel stereotypes. For example, Graham (2006) found that schools with greater ethnic diversity often had fewer severe problems with racism as long as each racial group had access to power (both formally and informally) and a large enough representation within the population.

While intergroup contact (real or imagined) seems to be a common component of prejudice reduction programs for children, other approaches have also been shown to be beneficial. In one meta-analysis, researchers examined 32 studies of interventions designed to reduce ethnic prejudice in children under eight-years old (Aboud et al., 2012). They found more positive effects on changing attitudes than on changing peer relationships. Both media instruction and intergroup contact were effective, but more studies using media instruction resulted in positive changes. Some programs also use creative arts to facilitate prejudice reduction. For example, Bell (2009, 2010) uses narrative to encourage discussions about how to end racism by integrating storytelling into programs teaching children about race and ethnicity.

Educators can also draw on the results of research studies that have demonstrated the effectiveness of interventions to reduce prejudice against specific stigmatized groups. For example, Duke and McCarthy (2009) provide a list of strategies (developed based on a review of 31 research articles) for early education teachers that outlines how they can challenge homophobia in the school environment, as well as ways to promote gender equality. In my own research, I have examined the impact of the Fairness for All Individuals through Respect (FAIR) program on children's engagement in gender prejudice within the classroom (Brinkman, Jedinak, Rosén, & Zimmerman, 2011). The program, which utilizes experiential activities to teach children about fairness and gender stereotypes, decreases engagement in gender prejudice against peers (compared to a control group) and increases students' endorsement of gender equality.

Whole-School Approach

Many scholars recommend using a *whole-school approach* to understanding and preventing bullying (McNamara, 2013). Schools should address the individual, social, and environmental factors that can contribute to bullying (Swearer, Espelage, Vaillancourt, & Hymel, 2010). While there are likely common social and environmental factors across schools within a society, each school represents its own community with its unique strengths and challenges. In order for interventions to be optimally effective at preventing identity-based bullying, they should be adapted to be appropriate for that community. Individuals at each school need not start from scratch—they can utilize evidence-based recommendations while adjusting for the needs of their community. In order to do this, schools are encouraged to adopt theoretically driven programs that have an evidence base (Swearer et al., 2010). The challenge to doing this is that it is not always clear which aspects of research based programs makes them effective. Therefore, it is important for schools to have an assessment plan for their own implementation to ensure that the steps they are taking are working in their community.

Resources

There are numerous handbooks about bullying prevention and intervention that teachers, school counselors, administrators, and scholars may find helpful. These include *Bullying in American Schools* by Espelage and Swearer (2004), *The Anti-Bullying Handbook* by Sullivan (2011), *Bullying Prevention and Intervention: Realistic Strategies for Schools* by Swearer, Espelage, and Napolitano (2009) and others. Scholars have also written helpful books about ways to address specific types of identity-based bullying in schools, including sexism and homophobia (Dewitt, 2012; Meyer, 2009), racist bullying (Richardson & Miles, 2008), and bullying of students with disabilities (McNamara, 2013). There are also countless organizations, nonprofit groups, and special interest groups that have developed their own approach to bullying prevention or are devoted to decreasing discrimination and securing equality and justice for all children. For example, Dan Savage, LGBT advocate and sex columnist, started the *It Gets Better* project to support LGBT youth who were being bullied or who otherwise felt alone (see Appendix). The campaign started as a website where individuals could upload videos describing their experiences. The website has over 10,000 videos, including videos by actors, athletes, and politicians. In March 2011, Savage and Miller published *It Gets Better: Coming Out, Overcoming Bullying, and Creating a Life Worth Living* in which they write, "The point of the project is to give despairing LGBT kids *hope*" (p. 8) (see the Appendix for more information about programs and organizations addressing identity-based bullying and related topics).

TEAM BUILDING AND STRATEGIC PLANNING

Schools are encouraged to assemble teams to focus on identity-based bullying within their communities. Utilizing a team, rather than relying on one or two individuals to design and implement policies and programs, can lead to a more expansive and comprehensive approach. It is important to carefully consider the composition of this team, and Anderson (2011) recommends they include a heterogeneous group of school staff, students, and community members. In addition to reaching out to parents and others who are already connected to the schools, administrators can collaborate with scholars or mental health professionals who have expertise in promoting diversity and decreasing identity-based bullying. Ideally, the team will include individuals with a range of social identities in terms of gender, ethnicity, social class, sexual orientation, and ability status. Such diversity assures that voices from marginalized groups have representation within the process and can help the team engage in better decision making (Hong & Page, 2004). While it is may not be feasible to directly represent all identities and perspectives that are present within the community, it is important to consider which voices are present and the implications this may have for interventions. The team should consider what it can do to integrate perspectives that are absent. They can educate themselves about other worldviews and experiences (through readings, films, experiential activities) and invite others to do specific tasks for the team (such as review a survey or interview questions or read over the team's final recommendations).

Strategic Planning

Once a team is formed, they can use strategic planning to assess the current climate and develop interventions to identity-based bullying within a school. Strauss (2012) recommends numerous steps to develop a strategic plan. I have adapted them here into a seven-step plan:

1. Develop a vision for the desired school environment
2. Assess the current environment
3. Describe gaps between the desired and current environment
4. Identify supports and barriers to closing the gaps
5. Develop an action plan with measurable goals
6. Implement the plan
7. Assess and revise

As with any strategic planning process, individuals will likely engage in a back-and-forth process of considering the big picture and working out specific logistics. The first step of developing a vision is essential but may be overlooked if team members assume that they all know what they are working toward. However, the vision for the school is crucial in shaping the strategic plan. For example, the approach that a team takes to design an intervention to punish identity-based bullying may differ drastically from an intervention designed to create a safe, inclusive environment. Even when schools explicitly discuss their vision, they might develop limited goals for themselves out of a concern that they cannot achieve something bigger. Unfortunately, setting pessimistic goals or assuming that schools cannot make systemic changes will surely prevent them from doing so. This does not mean that a team needs to tackle everything at once. The team can build a vision of education that supports the development of a diverse and inclusive society and then focus on making step-by-step changes that will move the school in the direction of their desired end.

Once the team has outlined their desired school environment, they need to assess the current environment and describe the discrepancies between the two. They should generate a comprehensive list of what areas need to change in order to eradicate identity-based bullying from their school. The team should develop a plan to examine the individual factors that may promote or deter (directly and indirectly) identity-based bullying. Meyer (2009, p. 63) provides a useful model that schools can utilize to examine the various external and internal influences that contribute to gendered harassment in schools—this model can easily be expanded to consider all types of identity-based bullying.

After making a list of the desired areas of change and the factors in place that would support and challenge that change, the team should prioritize targets for both short-term and long-term plans. If there is a lot of pessimism, it may be helpful to start with a problem that seems most responsive to intervention. Addressing a problem successfully can produce small victories that the team can build upon, boosts confidence of the staff in their ability to generate change, and begins to create a culture shift in the school. Meyer (2009) provides a list of activities that individuals within school systems can engage in to combat gendered harassment and bullying that she labels *low risk*, *some risk*, or *greater risk* to acknowledge that activities that will help to combat discrimination require varying degrees of vulnerability on the part of change agents. Teams may use this type of categorizing system to decide what steps to take first, often starting at low risk and building confidence and gathering allies with each action. Other teams may decide to start with the problem that is most prevalent in the school, address an issue that already has some momentum, or may use other criteria to determine the priority. However the team decides to do so, setting reasonable and measurable goals will help schools take steps toward their vision.

Once an intervention has been developed, the team should assess the outcomes and be willing to make changes when the evidence suggests they are needed. Schools may develop some site-specific surveys but should also consider using assessment tools that are available to them through the research literature. For example, Nickerson, Aloe, and Livingston (2014) developed a measure for schools interested in assessing whether their programming influences bystander intervention for both bullying and sexual harassment. Regardless of how they are developed, all assessment and intervention tools should be accessible to students who have disabilities (see McNamara, 2013 for a comprehensive list of ways to make accommodations) and use inclusive language in regard to gender, ethnicity, sexual orientation, and social class.

PUTTING RECOMMENDATIONS INTO ACTION

In this section, I provide a number of general recommendations for effective approaches to eradicating identity-based bullying. The recommendations are based on compilations of research studies about deterring bullying and discrimination in schools. I use three case examples to explore how these recommendations can be put into action. The cases are not based on any one student but rather are fictional vignettes based on the stories of numerous children in similar scenarios.

Recommendations:

1. Appropriately label identity-based bullying and differentiate it from other forms of bullying or harassment
2. Engage multiple stakeholders
3. Focus on prevention and proactive strategies
4. Assess and be willing to change the school environment
5. Examine societal and cultural influences on identity-based bullying

Case One: Adila—a 16-year-old Muslim girl who wears a hijab—recently transferred into a new school. On her first day of school, a classmate approached her and asked, "Why are you wearing a towel on your head? Did you forget to take it off after you showered?" The classmate and a handful of other students laughed and pointed at Adila. Adila began crying and ran out of the room. The teacher called after her and said that if she left the room without a hall pass, she would go to detention. Adila explained to her teacher what happened and was told to return to her seat. The next day (and on most days), students whispered "towel head" as they passed Adila in the hallway.

Case Two: Billy is an 11-year-old Black boy who has always loved dance, fashion, and the color pink. In the past, these interests were encouraged by his teacher who worked to develop a gender-inclusive classroom. His classmates barely noted Billy's interests—everyone liked what they liked. This year Billy is in a class with a new teacher, and his class cohort has been mixed with a few others. Billy's mom suspected that something was wrong after just a few weeks into the new school year. Before this year, Billy had always loved school and often talked about how much he looked forward to going, but suddenly he was asking to stay at home or telling his mom that he was too sick to go to school. After a few weeks, Billy's mom asked him what was wrong. He started crying and told her that three new boys at school had been teasing him. They told him that dancing is for girls and only *sissy boys* like pink. Billy's mom called the school to talk to his teacher, and during the conversation she learned that Billy's new teacher told Billy to stop playing with the girls, to "be a man," and to defend himself to the other boys.

Case Three: Alice is a 14-year-old White girl from a working class family that sometimes struggles to make ends meet. Alice has one older brother and she often wears his hand-me down clothes. She doesn't mind because she feels more comfortable in jeans and T-shirts than dresses. But it still stings when the other girls make fun of her clothes and her hairstyle, calling her names such as *chav* or *white trash*. She hates going to physical education because the other girls often tease her in the locker room. She had ignored them until one Monday when she showed up to school and found the word *slut* had been painted on her locker. She fought back tears as she gathered her books for the day and hurried to hide in a bathroom stall where no one could see her cry. In the bathroom, she overheard a classmate say, "Haven't you heard? Alice totally had sex with Dylan at the party on Saturday. What a slut!" Alice couldn't believe it—she hadn't even gone to the party. She did have a crush on Dylan and was thinking about asking him to the next dance, but now she was too humiliated. Since that day, she has been getting sexually explicit messages on Facebook from unknown people, hears people whisper "slut" when she walks by, and sees boys make obscene gestures when she passes them in the hallway.

Appropriately Label Identity-Based Bullying and Differentiate it from Other Forms of Bullying or Harassment

As noted in Chapter 6, in order for individuals to engage in bystander intervention, they must first label behavior as identity-based bullying. Some behavior that occurs within schools goes unaddressed because it is seen as normal or acceptable. For example, in Billy's case, the teacher has internalized traditional stereotypes about masculinity and is neglecting to appropriately address the identity-based bullying Billy is experiencing in the classroom. Instead, Billy's teacher is reinforcing the stereotypes about masculinity. This may occur within many schools, as the "practices of normalised masculine violence, which we may wish to challenge as oppressive, are defined outside the purview of the bully discourse" (Ringrose & Renold, 2010, p. 584). In order for adult educators (like Billy's teacher) to be proactive in addressing identity-based bullying, they must first shift their own paradigms.

One of the challenges often facing school officials is the need to understand the overlap between identity-based bullying and other forms of harassment and discrimination. Unfortunately, in many cases, it appears that this overlap leads to confusion and inaction. Many school educators in the U.S. appear to be unaware of the legal obligations they have for protecting students against discrimination and harassment based on aspects of social identity (Meyer, 2009). However, if schools proactively discuss the important distinctions between identity-based bullying and harassment and discrimination, teachers and those adults interacting directly with students in schools will be better equipped to appropriately label the behavior. As addressed in Chapter 6, labeling is important because it helps community members take the best action when a problem occurs. It is the first step to ensuring that schools follow legal requirements to both report and protect students from discrimination. Further, recognizing that identity-based bullying is one form of discrimination that occurs within a school may help educators realize that other types of discrimination related to that aspect of identity may be transpiring as well.

In Alice's case, she is experiencing sexual harassment in addition to class-based and gender-based bullying. In the U.S., students have a right to be protected from sexual harassment based on title IX, but many schools do not take this seriously (Pascoe, 2007). Even schools that do have policies about and take action against sexual harassment may not always recognize the extent of behaviors that are included in this definition. *Slut shaming*—experiences where a girl is called a slut and/or is teased and harassed about her real or rumored engagement in sexual activity (Ringrose, 2013)—may be minimized by school officials. Educators may not identify this behavior as being problematic (let alone label it is as identity-based bullying or harassment) as many adults take for granted the everyday acts that children engage in to enforce expectations about (hetero)sexuality (Renold, 2002). In other cases, a school may recognize slut shaming but treat it as an act of bullying during which they assume the problem exists between particular girls. In these cases, schools may punish the girls involved in the bullying without exploring or understanding (or working to change) the larger problems within the school. However, it is likely that slut shaming occurring within a school is related to larger cultural problems about the treatment of girls/women within that school. Sexual harassment and gender-based bullying can be one way that children police each other's behaviors to ensure they fit into internalized gender and sexual norms (Renold, 2005). Slut shaming may be indicative of a climate in which girls are objectified and sexualized, where girls are held responsible and accountable for boys' sexual behavior, and possibly a climate that reinforces rape culture and tolerates sexual assault. By labeling slut shaming as a form of sexual harassment (in addition to being identity-based bullying), schools not only do what is best for the target but will be better positioned to explore the factors occurring within the school that may be contributing to this phenomenon.

Engage Multiple Stakeholders

Efforts to detect, prevent, and respond to identity-based bullying within schools will be most effective if they engage multiple stakeholders within the community. This includes students, teachers, staff, administrators, parents, and possibly scholars or mental health professionals from the community. In Chapter 6, I describe some of the barriers to engaging students in identity-based bullying prevention and intervention. Addressing those challenges is essential, as children and adolescents can play a critical role in effectively deterring identity-based bullying. Engaging these stakeholders means ensuring that they have real power to contribute to decision making (particularly students whose voices may often be minimized). Even those members of the community who may not be on a schools' official "response team" should be included to assess the strengths of a school and to recognize the areas in need of improvement (Orpinas & Horne, 2006). For example, teachers can help identify the values of the school, ways they are broken, and methods to address value violations (Orpinas & Horne, 2006).

It is important to both include the perspectives of those who have been disenfranchised while utilizing the power of social capital to make interventions effective. The culture of a school can be changed if a few individuals with social capital support these changes (Fried & Soslan, 2011). Programs that get favorite teachers and popular students on board can be especially impactful. Sullivan (2011) suggests that schools can call upon various types of leaders to engage in anti-bullying efforts. Many school officials will likely be quick to recommend those students they see as being positive leaders, but Sullivan (2011) argues that schools should also include students who may engage in "negative" leadership styles (including students who may be labeled *bullies*) in peer support programs. If these students can learn to harness their leadership potential in ways that support the values of the school and provide for positive interactions with their peers and teachers, they can play a powerful role in combating identity-based bullying.

Children who witness others being targeted with identity-based bullying may engage in behaviors as bystanders who inadvertently or directly support the mistreatment by being a follower, supporter, passive supporter, or disengaged onlooker (Strauss, 2012). Teaching students how to be proactive bystanders when they observe harassment and identity-based bullying is one way to increase intervention. One meta-analysis examined 11 studies (including over 12,000 students) and found that programs focused on increasing bystander intervention were generally effective at doing so in ways that had both statistical and practical significance (Polanin, Espelage, & Pigott, 2012). In my work examining children's (ages 8–12) intended responses to gender-based bullying, more than 75% of the students indicated they would want to use an assertive response as a bystander, such as confronting the perpetrator or getting help from an adult (Brinkman & Manning, in press). While this finding is hopeful, the students also described seven types of barriers that might prevent them from actually using such an assertive response. Understanding students' desires to be proactive bystanders but also being aware of the barriers to doing so is crucial when developing interventions. Educators should directly address these barriers with children and brainstorm ways to counter them.

One of the common barriers to bystander intervention reported by children is adults—including the perception that adults will not help even when asked. In one study, 25% of 631 children surveyed reported they felt teachers did little to stop bullying (Slee, 2003). These studies (and others) indicate that teachers are sometimes silent bystanders to identity-based bullying. In Chapter 6, I describe ways teachers can be more proactive bystanders in the decision-making process when an identity-based bullying incident occurs. However, there are also things that educators can do even before an event occurs, during the time Anderson (2011) calls the *pre-bystanderism stage*. During this phase, teachers and administrators are encouraged to engage in self-reflection to examine their beliefs about aspects of social identity and become more aware of blinds spots they may have that could prevent them from recognizing identity-based bullying. They can then cultivate the skills to be able to notice when something unusual is going on in their schools. In Billy's case, his new teacher may need to engage in some work to examine her internalized ideas about masculinity. The school should be sure it has a policy about gender-based bullying and that the new teacher understands when and how this policy applies. The new teacher could also receive some mentoring from Billy's previous teachers and other educators in the school who have employed strategies for gender inclusive teaching.

In Billy's case, it may be helpful to use a classroom-wide or school-wide program addressing gender-role stereotypes and emphasizing the importance of treating everyone with respect and dignity. Many scholars have noted that most boys feel pressure to conform to traditional gender stereotypes (e.g., Kimmel & Mahler, 2003; Pollack, 1999) and may suppress interests or avoid displaying personality characteristics that do not meet these expectations. Thus, although Billy may be disproportionately targeted for bullying, there are likely other boys in the classroom who worry that they may face the same treatment if they behave authentically (especially if that authenticity is counter to hegemonic masculinity). Utilizing programs such as Fairness for All Individuals through Respect (FAIR) and Coaching Boys into Men (see Appendix) can encourage all children in the class (or school) to examine stereotypical gender expectations. The boys can decide to work together to decrease pressure to conform and advocate for all children to be able to behave authentically. In one school where I administered the FAIR program, one of the more popular fifth-grade boys disclosed his feelings of stress related to expectations to fit into traditional masculinity norms. He worried that if he stopped playing football or had a bad day, he would be teased. At the end of the program, he talked about the possibility of breaking out of gender-role norms and advocated for everyone in the class to support others in behaving authentically, even if they acted counter to gender stereotypes (see Brinkman et al., 2011 for more information about this study).

Focus on Prevention and Proactive Strategies

Schools taking a social justice approach to deter identity-based bullying should differentiate between reactive strategies (those that are designed to address an event that has already occurred) and proactive strategies (those that anticipate possible problems or challenges). Focusing on prevention and proactive approaches will increase the likelihood that all members of the community feel safe. Educators can be proactive in preventing identity-based bullying by having positive expectations of the students, including having students demonstrate care and respect for other community members (Orpinas & Horne, 2006). Schools can emphasize prevention of identity-based bullying by encouraging behaviors that promote positive, supportive, and inclusive relationships and reinforcing acts of kindness among students (McNamara, 2013). Schools should also assess for and celebrate their own strengths—noticing what they do well as a community and building upon that foundation.

One proactive strategy that schools can embrace is to utilize a social justice and antiracist curriculum that provides students with current and historical information about social identities, while also fostering deep discussions about these issues. In Adila's case, education about Islam, its customs, and beliefs may be helpful to address stereotypes that might be pervasive within the school (and held by students, teachers, and parents). Dewitt (2012) discusses how teachers can introduce discussions about LGBT individuals and rights through the curriculum they develop. Teachers can assign age-appropriate literature that includes LGBT characters or encourages discussions about gender norms, they can teach about legal and policy battles for LGBT rights within social studies, and include gay artists in music or art classes. Organizations such as the Anti-Defamation League and Teaching Tolerance (see Appendix) provide social justice curriculum guides, classroom resources, and support for professional development for educators.

A proactive approach to deterring identity-based bullying also involves looking for ways to turn incidents into teachable moments to support larger cultural changes and prevent future incidents. Anderson (2011) refers to this as the *post-bystanderism* stage. Rather than simply stopping the behavior in question, in this stage educators try to make the experience a learning opportunity for the students involved as well as others in the school. In my own work at a therapeutic boarding school for boys, I often utilized this approach. The school had an active outdoor recreation program, so we spent a lot of time playing games at city parks. It was common for the boys to get into arguments while playing capture the flag or ultimate Frisbee and resort to verbal insults. Almost always, this barrage included some version of "Yeah, well you throw like a girl!" Being a woman who was also playing the game, I was offended by this comment and said so. Mostly, the boys were surprised that I was insulted by their remarks. They had internalized the belief that the worst way to offend a boy was to call him a girl without considering what these statements implied about females. In addition to managing the conflict at hand, I tried to use the incidents as teachable moments to challenge stereotypes about masculinity. I utilized other proactive strategies at the school to encourage conversations about masculinity, social class, ethnicity, and other aspects of identity. I started a social issues group and brought in newspaper clippings about current events related to ethnicity, social class, and gender stereotypes and took the children on field trips to films and public lectures about diversity.

Although I encourage schools to emphasize prevention, it is important for educators to consider how to best respond when identity-based bullying occurs. Educators utilizing a social justice framework should prioritize restorative justice over punitive goals. Many schools utilize punitive approaches in which a behavior is viewed as a violation of a rule where the goal is to punish the offender. In contrast, restorative justice views an offense as a violation of a relationship (see Richardson & Miles, 2008 for a comparison of punitive and restorative justice approaches as they relate to racism in schools). Restorative justice emphasizes repairing the harm that has been caused by someone's behavior (Van Ness & Strong, 2015). From a restorative justice context, the victim, the offender, and the entire community are stakeholders in repairing the damage that was caused by someone's actions (Zehr, 2002). These approaches seem especially relevant when dealing with identity-based bullying because they recognize that the behaviors can harm everyone within a community, not just those directly involved in a single incident. Restorative justice approaches to handling identity-based bullying can serve to heal those impacted by the behavior, while also working to create a more just and inclusive environment. While being clear that certain behaviors are not tolerated within an environment is an important step, an entirely punitive approach to addressing identity-based bullying is not as effective as an approach that seeks to create a just and fair environment.

Assess and be Willing to Change the School Environment

A school climate and culture that values diversity of ethnicity, social class, gender, sexual orientation, and ability status and promotes equity for all individuals is something all members of that school can actively work toward creating. Achieving such an environment may involve targeting and working to eradicate behaviors that conflict with the values of the school but goes beyond this. Rather than attempting to develop policies that define problems and punishments under all circumstances, schools should be willing to continually assess and change the school environment for the better. In some schools, this may require a shift in thinking from an approach that emphasizes changing the way the victim behaves (e.g., how to confront bullies) to an approach that emphasizes how school environments should change to decrease bullying (Klein, 2012).

Hinduja and Patchin (2012) assert that to completely understand how the school environment reinforces bullying, educators should examine the social environment, affective environment, academic environment, and physical environment. Their suggestions on how schools can improve all aspects of their environment in order to create a bully-free school climate can be adapted to eradicate identity-based bullying. A social environment that promotes cooperation and healthy interactions includes friendly staff who get along with each other; shared decision making with input from students, teachers, and administration; and workshops about ways to prevent identity-based bullying. An affective environment that promotes a sense of belonging and helps students develop their self-esteem demonstrates trust between students and staff, high morale, a sense of community, investment in the school, and valuing of diversity. An academic environment that promotes learning encourages academics, uses teaching methods that recognize that students learn in a variety of ways, and uses assessment to adjust and improve teaching methods. Finally, schools should take into consideration ways that the physical environment may encourage identity-based bullying and be willing to change the environment to be a safer space for all children.

In all three of the case examples, schools could better address identity-based bullying that occurs by assessing the school environment and looking for ways to create change. The social environment of each school could be improved by better attending to gender, sexual orientation, social class, ethnicity, and religion. Schools with younger children should consider deemphasizing gender differences and using inclusive language when discussing romantic relationships. For example, in Billy's case, the teacher asserts that Billy shouldn't play with the girls' toys, implying that there are separate toys/activities for boys and girls. Schools can train educators not to utilize gender as a primary way of grouping children and their activities, but to use other ways to organize them (i.e., favorite color, birth month, etc.). Teachers should use inclusive language when talking about parents and families and not assume that the children themselves will grow up to be heterosexual, nor assume that all children have heterosexual parents. Schools with older children can work to eradicate identity-based bullying of students who are LGBT or who do not conform to gender stereotypes by implementing programs and assemblies about gender and sexual orientation and altering the school environment to be supportive of nonheteronormative expressions of gender and sexuality (Pascoe, 2007). For example, educators should change policies that encourage heterosexuality and traditional gender expressions, such as policies about who can be homecoming king and queen, bans on same-sex couples attending dances, and the use of heterosexist and/or homophobic language.

Schools can also work to shift the affective environment through the use of clubs and empowerment groups. Many schools have implemented Gay-Straight Alliances (GSAs), which encourage interactions between LGBT students and allies. Some scholars have found that the presence of a GSA in a school can have numerous benefits, including decreased victimization of LGBTQ students (Toomey, Ryan, Diaz, & Russell, 2011) and creation of a safer and more inclusive environment (Dewitt, 2012). GSAs may offer benefits even for those LGBTQ students who do not join them, as they promote a positive representation of their identity within the school (Poteat, Sinclair, DiGiovanni, Koenig, & Russell, 2013). Clubs, student organizations, and empowering groups can be developed to foster more supportive environments related to other aspects of identity as well. In one school, educators developed and implemented transformative groups for seventh and eighth graders who were students of color attending a school with limited resources (Shin et al., 2010). The groups were designed to empower students through sociopolitical education and consciousness-raising. The leaders strove to address internalized stereotypes, as well as institutional oppression. This approach worked to affirm the members of the group and utilized education to combat internalized oppression and to confront systemic barriers within the school. These types of groups may be beneficial for students of color (like Billy) and students from working class families (like Alice) by providing them with support and resources.

The academic environment can be improved by encouraging excellence in teaching and expecting teachers and other educators to be knowledgeable about diversity so they can integrate social issues into their own teaching/intervention efforts. Creating a positive school environment also requires providing support for teachers and ongoing development of the staff (Orpinas & Horne, 2006). Talking about issues of social identity can be challenging for some adults, especially if they are being asked to be more aware of their own prejudices (Duke & McCarthy, 2009). Richardson and Miles (2008) provide a useful framework and numerous activities that can be used to train teachers and staff about issues related to race/ethnicity. They argue that effective training can only happen when individuals acknowledge that discussions about race/ethnicity are often sensitive and sometimes controversial. Rather than attempting to ignore these facts, they encourage participants in workshops to find productive ways to validate each other's complex experiences of race/ethnicity and to be open to learning. Similarly, Dessel (2010) describes the use of intergroup dialogues to positively change public school teachers' attitudes about the LGB community. Other scholars suggest that teachers can develop multicultural awareness regarding sexual orientation by engaging in continuing education that combines factual information, structured activities, and small group discussions (Walters & Hayes, 1998). While these approaches have been designed for specific topics, the same principles may be useful for training educators about any social identity.

Examine Societal and Cultural Influences on Identity-Based Bullying

Schools may be able to more effectively prevent identity-based bullying if they examine the societal and cultural influences on children within their communities. While prosocial approaches to addressing bullying may encourage children to treat people more fairly or to challenge unfair treatment, it may not be as effective in challenging the deeper structures that support and sustain identity-based bullying. Pahlke, Bigler, and Martin (2014) found that children in programs that taught egalitarian attitudes (that one should challenge sexism and stereotypes) were more likely to recognize sexism in the media and used more antisexist challenges to hypothetical scenarios than children in programs with a prosocial approach (i.e., it is not nice to tease others). The final recommendation I pose for addressing identity-based bullying is to examine how cultural influences outside of the school are impacting the dynamics taking place within the school. In many ways, this is a key argument of this book—that a social justice approach to eradicating identity-based bullying requires exploring the ways this phenomenon is impacted by larger social issues.

Schools can implement a range of programming that provides children and adolescents with tools to examine cultural messages about gender, ethnicity, social class, sexual orientation, ability, and other aspects of identity. In Alice's case, groups that encourage girls to challenge media messages and stereotypes about gender may help her and other girls in her school dissect messages related to girls' sexuality and sexual harassment. Some programs promote students working together to improve the school environment, while also challenging larger cultural messages about identity. For example, Hardy Girls Healthy Women provides curriculum for Girls Coalition Groups designed for girls in the fourth through eighth grades (see Appendix for more information). The groups meet weekly in schools and engage in media literacy, discussions about ways to be an ally to other girls, and education about proactively changing their own school culture to increase gender equality. These types of programs can also teach students media literacy skills, which can be used to critique the portrayal or representation of groups of people or social identities (Radeloff & Bergman, 2009). Schools can offer media literacy courses, integrate media literacy training into existing courses in English or the social sciences, or offer workshops and programming focused on media literacy. Groups such as The Representation Project (see Appendix) offer films and curriculum for schools to engage students in critical thinking about gender stereotypes. Students can also participate in activities and programs that promote the development of a civic identity and engagement in activism. Adult educators can encourage youth to join social change movements, which provide numerous educational opportunities for children and adolescents (Kirshner, 2007). For example, the organization SPARK (Sexualization Protest: Action, Resistance, Knowledge; see Appendix) supports girl activism through participation in online forums, blogs, and protest marches related to the sexualization of women (Edell, Brown, & Tolman, 2013). Schools can integrate some of the SPARK curriculum into their own work and/or encourage girls and young women to get involved directly and become a member of their action squad.

In addition to implementing long-term programs that shift cultural attitudes about gender, sexual orientation, social class, ethnicity, etc., schools can be proactive about recognizing dynamics that may occur within their schools following current events. For example, incidents of anti-Muslim harassment and violence often increase following incidents of terrorism by Muslims. In January 2015, Muslims around the United Kingdom reported backlash and increased harassment following the terrorist attack on the French magazine *Charlie Hebdo*—the magazine had been targeted for publishing cartoons of the Prophet Mohamed (Milmo, 2015). A charity monitoring anti-Muslim hate crimes within the U.K. found a significant increase in reports following the event, including incidents where children within schools were slapped and called *terrorist* (Milmo, 2015). Educators should identify the possibility that their Muslim students, Arab students, and other students who are perceived to be from the Middle East may become targets of increased identity-based bullying and harassment following such events. For example, Adila's school should be alert to possible mistreatment following events like the one in Paris. Schools should take a proactive stance when such events occur by having discussions with students about the event, how they feel about the event, and what they are hearing about the event at home and at school. It is more important than ever in such critical times for schools to convey their expectations to students about how to treat each other and to provide opportunities for thoughtful discussions.

CONCLUSION

In many ways, this was the most challenging chapter of the book to write. I found myself continually wanting to provide readers with all the answers (or maybe the *best* answers). I want to offer an easy-to-use, step-by-step formula for eradicating identity-based bullying, but I had to remind myself that such a thing does not exist. Instead, I provide general recommendations and tips for best practices based on the body of research available. Although many of my recommendations have focused on those already working within a school environment, it is important to note that training to prevent and respond to identity-based bullying can (and should) start with the education of teachers, school counselors, and administrators. It is my hope that this chapter provides educators with some guidance to address a large and complex issue. While at times it may seem that the problem is too big to solve, I encourage educators to celebrate even the smallest victories—knowing that sometimes change happens like an avalanche and sometimes change results from the slow accumulation of tiny beautiful snowflakes.

REFERENCES

Abbott, N., & Cameron, L. (2014). What makes a young assertive bystander? The effect of intergroup contact, empathy, cultural openness, and in-group bias on assertive bystander intervention intentions. *Journal of Social Issues, 70*, 167–182. doi: 10.1111/josi.12053

Aboud, F. E., Tredoux, C., Tropp, L. R., Brown, C. S., Niens, U., Noor, N. M., & the UN Global Evaluation Group. (2012). Interventions to reduce prejudice and enhance inclusion and respect for ethnic differences in early childhood: A systematic review. *Developmental Review, 32*, 307–336. doi: 10.1016/j.dr.2012.05.001

Anderson, S. (2011). *No more bystanders = no more bullies: Activating action in educational professionals.* Thousand Oaks, CA: Corwin.

Beelmann, A., & Heinemann, K. S. (2014). Preventing prejudice and improving intergroup attitudes: A meta-analysis of child and adolescent training programs. *Journal of Applied Developmental Psychology, 35*, 10–24. doi: 10.1016/j.appdev.2013.11.002

Bell, L. A. (2009). The story of the storytelling project: An arts-based race and social justice curriculum. *Storytelling, Self, Society: An Interdisciplinary Journal of Storytelling Studies, 5,* 107–118.

Bell, L. A. (2010). *Storytelling for social justice: Connecting narrative and the arts in antiracist teaching.* New York: Routledge Press.

Brinkman, B. G., Jedinak, A., Rosén, L. A., & Zimmerman, T. S. (2011). Teaching children fairness: Decreasing gender prejudice among children. *Analyses of Social Issues and Public Policy, 11,* 61–81. doi: 10.1111/j.1530-2415.2010.01222.x

Brinkman, B. G., & Manning, L. (in press). Children's intended responses to gender-based bullying as targets and bystanders. *Childhood.*

Cameron, L., Rutland, A., & Brown, R. (2007). Promoting children's positive intergroup attitudes towards stigmatized groups: Extended contact and multiple classification skills training. *International Journal of Behavioral Development, 31,* 454–466. doi: 10.1177/0165025407081474

Dessel, A. (2010). Effects of intergroup dialogue: Public school teachers and sexual orientation prejudice. *Small Group Research, 41,* 556–592.

Dewitt, P. (2012). *Dignity for all: Safeguarding LGBT students.* London, UK: Corwin.

Duke, T. S., & McCarthy, K. W. (2009). Homophobia, sexism and early childhood education: A review of the literature. *Journal of Early Childhood Teacher Education, 30,* 385–403. doi: 10.1080/10901020903320320

Edell, D., Brown, L.M., & Tolman, D. (2013). Embodying sexualisation: When theory meets practice in intergenerational feminist activism. *Feminist Theory, 14,* 275–284. doi: 10.1177/1464700113499844

Espelage, D.L., & Swearer, S.M. (2004). *Bullying in American schools: A social-ecological perspective on prevention and intervention.* Mahwah, NJ: Lawrence Erlbaum Associates.

Fried, S., & Soslan, B. (2011). *Banishing bullying behavior: Transforming the culture of peer abuse* (2nd ed.). Lanham, MD: Rowman & Littlefield Education.

Graham, S. (2006). Peer victimization in school: Exploring the ethnic context. *Current Directions in Psychological Science, 15,* 317–321. doi: 10.1111/j.1467-8721.2006.00460.x

Hewstone, M., & Swart, H. (2011). Fifty-odd years of inter-group contact: From hypothesis to integrated theory. *British Journal of Social Psychology, 50,* 374–386. doi: 10.1111/j.2044-8309.2011.02047.x

Hinduja, S., & Patchin, J.W. (2012). *School climate 2.0: Preventing cyberbullying and sexting one classroom at a time.* Thousand Oaks, CA: Corwin.

Hong, L., & Page, S.E. (2004). Groups of diverse problem solvers can outperform groups of high-ability problem solvers. *PNAS, 101,* 16385–16389.

Kimmel, M. S., & Mahler, M. (2003). Adolescent masculinity, homophobia, and violence: Random school shootings, 1982–2001. *American Behavioral Scientist, 46,* 1439–1458. doi: 10.1177/0002764203046010010

Kirshner, B. (2007). Youth activism as a context for learning and development. *American Behavioral Scientist, 51,* 367–379. doi: 10.1177/0002764207306065

Klein, J. (2012). *The bully society: School shootings and the crisis of bullying in America's schools.* New York, NY: New York University Press.

McNamara, B.E. (2013). *Bullying and students with disabilities: Strategies and techniques to create a safe learning environment for all.* Thousand Oaks, CA: Corwin.

Merrell, K. W., Gueldner, B. A., Ross, S. C., Isava, D.M. (2008). How effective are school bullying intervention programs? A meta-analysis of intervention research. *School Psychology Review, 23,* 26–42.

Meyer, E. J. (2009). *Gender, bullying, and harassment: Strategies to end sexism and homophobia in schools.* New York, NY: Teacher's College Press.

Milmo, C. (2015, January 23). British Muslim school children suffering a backlash of abuse following Paris attacks. *The Independent*. Retrieved from http://www.independent.co.uk/news/education/education-news/british-muslim-school-children-suffering-a-backlash-of-abuse-following-paris-attacks-9999393.html

Nelson, E. S., & Krieger, S. L. (1997). Changes in attitudes toward homosexuality in college students: Implementation of a gay men and lesbian peer panel. *Journal of Homosexuality, 33*, 63–81.

Nickerson, A. B., Aloe, A. M., & Livingston, J. A. (2014). Measurement of the bystander intervention model for bullying and sexual harassment. *Journal of Adolescence, 37*, 391–400.

Orpinas, P., & Horne, A. M. (2006). *Bullying Prevention: Creating a positive school climate and developing social competencies*. Washington, DC: American Psychological Association.

Pahlke, E., Bigler, R. S., & Martin, C. L. (2014). Can fostering children's ability to challenge sexism improve critical analysis, internalization, and enactment of inclusive, egalitarian peer relationships? *Journal of Social Issues, 70*, 115–133. doi: 10.1111/josi.12050

Pascoe, C. J. (2007). *Dude, you're a fag: Masculinity and sexuality in high school*. Berkley, CA: University of California Press.

Pettigrew, T. F. (1998). Intergroup contact theory. *Annual Review of Psychology, 49*, 65–85.

Pettigrew, T. F., & Tropp, L. R. (2006). A meta-analytic test of intergroup contact theory. *Journal of Personality and Social Psychology, 90*, 751–783. Retrieved from http://dx.doi.org/10.1037/0022-3514.90.5.751

Polanin, J. R., Espelage, D. L., & Pigott, T. D. (2012). A meta-analysis of school-based bullying prevention programs' effects on bystander intervention behavior. *School Psychology Review, 41*, 47–65.

Pollack, W. (1999). The sacrifice of Isaac: Toward a new psychology of boys and men. *The Society for the Psychological Study of Men and Masculinity, 4*, 7–14.

Poteat, V. P., Sinclair, K. O., DiGiovanni, C. D., Koenig, B. W., & Russell, S. T. (2013). Gay–Straight Alliances are associated with student health: A multischool comparison of LGBTQ and heterosexual youth. *Journal of Research on Adolescence, 23*, 319–330. doi: 10.1111/j.1532-7795.2012.00832.x

Radeloff, C. L., & Bergman, B. J. (2009). Global perspectives: Developing media literacy skills to advance critical thinking. *Feminist Teacher, 19*, 168–171.

Renold, E. (2002). 'Presumed innocence': (hetero)sexual, homophobic and heterosexist harassment amongst primary school girls and boys, *Childhood, 9*, 415–433.

Renold, E. (2005). *Girls, boys, and junior sexualities: Exploring children's gender and sexual relations in the primary school*. Routledge: London.

Richardson, R., & Miles, B. (2008). *Racist incidents and bullying in schools*. Staffordshire, UK: Trentham Books Limited.

Ringrose, J. (2013). *Postfeminist Education? Girls and the Sexual Politics of Schooling*. New York, NY: Routledge.

Ringrose, J., & Renold, E. (2010). Normative cruelties and gender deviants: The performative effects of bully discourses for girls and boys in school. *British Educational Research Journal, 36*, 573–596.

Savage, D., & Miller, T. (Eds.). (2011). *It Get's Better the book: Coming out, overcoming bullying, and creating a life worth living*. Dutton, New York.

Shin, R. Q., Rogers, J., Stanciu, A., Silas, M., Brown-Smythe, C., & Austin, B. (2010). Advancing social justice in urban schools through the implementation of transformative groups for youth of color. *The Journal for Specialists in Group Work, 35*, 230–235.

Slee, P. T. (2003). Bullying: A preliminary investigation of its nature and the effects of social cognition. *Early Child Development and Care, 87*, 47–57.

Smith, P. K., Salmivalli, C., & Cowie, H. (2012). Effectiveness of school-based programs to reduce bullying: A commentary. *Journal of Experiential Criminology, 8,* 433–441.
Strauss, S. (2012). *Sexual harassment and bullying: A guide to keeping kids safe and holding schools accountable.* Plymouth, UK: Rowman & Littlefield Publishers.
Sullivan, K. (2011). *The anti-bullying handbook* (2nd ed.). London, England: SAGE.
Swearer, S. M., Espelage, D. L., & Napolitano, S. A. (2009). *Bullying prevention and intervention: Realistic strategies for schools.* New York: Guilford Press.
Swearer, S. M., Espelage, D. L., Vaillancourt, T., & Hymel, S. (2010). What can be done about school bullying? Linking research to educational practice. *Educational Researcher, 39,* 38–47. doi: 10.3102/0013189X09357622
Toomey, R., Ryan, C., Diaz, R., & Russell, S. (2011). High school gay—straight alliances (GSAs) and young adult well-being: An examination of GSA presence, participation, and perceived effectiveness. *Applied Developmental Science, 15,* 175–185. doi: 10.1080/10888691.2011.607378
Van Ness, D. W., & Strong, K. H. (2015). *Restoring justice: An introduction to restorative justice.* Waltham, MA: Elsevier.
Walters, A. S., & Hayes, D. M. (1998). Homophobia within schools: Challenging the culturally sanctioned dismissal of gay students and colleagues. *Journal of Homosexuality, 35,* 1–23.
Yeager, D. S., Fong, C. J., Lee, H. Y., & Espelage, D. L. (2015). Declines in efficacy of anti-bullying programs among older adolescents: Theory and a three-level meta-analysis. *Journal of Applied Developmental Psychology, 37,* 36–51.
Zehr, H. (2002). *The little book of restorative justice.* Intercourse, PA: Good Books.

8 Conclusion

Writing this book has been a journey undertaken over multiple years. During that time, I often found myself working in public places, including coffee shops, libraries, and airports. Sometimes strangers who were interested in what I was doing interrupted me—they saw a book I was reading with the word *bullying* in it and felt compelled to chat with me. Perhaps not surprisingly, given the past seven chapters of this book and how they have described the broad impacts of bullying, many people had stories to share and questions to ask. Although sometimes I had to explain what I meant by social identities (class, ethnicity, gender, etc.), once I did, most people agreed right away that this element was imperative in effectively dealing with bullying.

One morning I was having breakfast at a coffee shop and catching up on a new book about bullying when a woman interrupted me (and apologized for doing so—Pittsburgh is filled with polite people) to ask why I was reading about bullying. I explained a bit about who I was and the book I was writing. She was also reading about bullying but for a very different reason. Her son had been bullied at school (she explained that he wasn't as "tough" as the other boys), and she felt like the school wasn't doing enough about it. She wanted to learn more and was hoping to offer a workshop to teach other parents about bullying. We talked for a brief time, and I made some suggestions for readings and gave her my business card. As I worked on this book, I often found myself thinking of that woman and her son, along with many others I met during that time who were brave enough to share their own stories with me. I do this work for them.

THE TAKE-HOME MESSAGE

The core argument of this book is that it is time for schools to take a new approach to deterring identity-based bullying, one that recognizes it as being both reflected in and influenced by cultural factors and situated within educational systems that often reproduce inequality. Messages sent to schools about what is (and is not) their role can greatly affect whether they are willing and able to tackle persistent injustices in schools related to gender, sexual orientation, social class, ethnicity, and other social identities. In an age of conversations and debates about school reforms, the quality of public schools, charter schools, and concerns about high-stakes testing, there seems to be little room for conversations about the true purpose of educating our children. Is the goal of public education to simply indoctrinate them into the ways of thinking and behaving that will allow them to survive current patriarchal, capitalist societies filled with social injustice? Or can it be something else entirely? I challenge all of us—scholars, educators, parents—to dream bigger. Let us see what happens when we conceptualize schools not as the mechanism for maintaining the status quo but instead as the epicenter for a social movement for a just and equitable society.

Many before me have asked similar questions and offered invaluable treatises on the deconstruction of traditional ideas of schooling and hopeful blueprints for more just alternatives. Freire's (1970) *Pedagogy of the Oppressed* and hooks's (1994) *Teaching to Transgress: Education as the Practice of Freedom* are classics that have greatly informed my own thinking about schooling. Numerous others have contributed to the canon on teaching for social justice—many of whom I have referred to in this work. The mission of approaching schooling in a "new" way is about the betterment of children and their lives in every aspect. As the Seeking Educational Equity and Diversity (SEED) project notes, "Curricula and teaching methods that are gender fair, multiculturally equitable, socioeconomically aware, and globally informed create the most effective learning environment for all students" (see the Appendix for more information about SEED). A curriculum that centers on social justice does not sacrifice effectiveness but rather creates the conditions necessary for learning and growth to occur.

In this book, I call upon teachers, school administrators, and mental health professionals to apply such a justice-oriented framework to the problem of bullying. Identity should be at the forefront of identity-based bullying prevention and intervention if for no other reason than the fact that many bullying incidents are related to aspects of social identity (Wessler & De Andrade, 2006). Children are targeted because of their gender identity (Brinkman, Jedinak, Rosén, & Zimmerman, 2011; Brown & Bigler, 2004; Meyer, 2009), sexual orientation (Meyer, 2009; Poteat & Espelage, 2005; Renold, 2005; Russell, Ryan, Toomey, Diaz, & Sanchez, 2011), ethnic identity (Richardson & Miles, 2008), and social class (Liu, Soleck, Hopps, Dunston, & Pickett, 2004). As a result, scholars have called for anti-bullying programs to pay more attention to aspects of identity (Jenson, Dieterich, Brisson, Bender, & Powell, 2010) and to differentiate between bullying and harassment (Brown, Chesney-Lind, & Stein, 2007; Meyer, 2009). In this book, I have examined the ways that bullying and harassment often overlap—drawing upon scholarship in both areas to provide a theoretical base as well as practical applications. Further, I assert that a social constructivist perspective will expand our thinking about how identity-based bullying impacts children's meaning making and identity development. I also encourage educators to move beyond labeling children as bully, victim, or bystander and instead embrace children and adolescents as active agents within their own lives, navigating complex dynamics and the politics of social relations. If we see children as potential change agents, not just recipients of programs, we can improve not only the lives of children who are being bullied but promote lasting social change.

Core to a social justice perspective on identity-based bullying is the examination of how contextual variables impact the development and continuation of this behavior. While most research about bullying has focused on individual characteristics that would lead a child to become a bully, I have emphasized how identity-based bullying stems from prejudice related to race, gender, social class, sexual orientation, religion, and ability. Children's engagement in identity-based bullying and how schools respond (or do not respond) are also heavily influenced by the structures of schooling, school environments, and educational laws and policies. For example, the rise of high-stakes testing in both the United Kingdom and the United States resulted in curriculum narrowing that has made it challenging for schools to address diversity and social justice topics (Farnen, 2007).

I have utilized an international perspective to describe how social, political, and contextual variables influence identity-based bullying. In particular, I have drawn upon scholarship and cultural events within the United States and the United Kingdom. These two nations have both similarities and distinctions in regard to cultural values about social identities, school structures, and laws and policies that apply to identity-based bullying. I have been diligent in my attempts to provide a balanced picture of these two nations. However, I am aware that as an American scholar I am better positioned to address the nuances within the United States than those within the United Kingdom. My research included extensive reading about how the United Kingdom has worked to integrate identity-based bullying prevention into its educational policies. However, written educational policies do not tell the entire picture of what actually occurs within schools. One report that compiled survey results of the local authorities in England, Scotland, and Wales about how their district were implementing programming to address identity-based bullying indicates that more research is needed to better understand the implementation and effectiveness of anti-bullying programs that target identity-based bullying (Tippett, Houlston, & Smith, 2010). Additional empirical research within these school systems and perspectives of insiders (both adults and children) will provide much-needed information about how policy meets (or does not meet) practice.

I acknowledge the challenges facing educators in their work to prevent and effectively intervene in identity-based bullying. There are no easy answers—even while writing this book I frequently faced this reality. People often asked what my book was about, and many of them shared their experiences with me (or those of their children, friends, and siblings). The hardest conversations for me were the ones in which someone sought advice for a current bullying situation. I did my best to share what I could and to offer support and guidance, but I often felt that those conversations were insufficient. There is no magic wand that will quickly and easily resolve the problem of identity-based bullying. While it can feel daunting to recognize the many barriers to this work, I truly believe that we can only begin to dismantle those barriers by naming them and developing a plan of action.

Finally, I have provided suggestions for best practices for teachers, administrators, and mental health professionals engaging in work to prevent identity-based bullying. I developed my recommendations by integrating the information available about how to best prevent bullying and how to deter prejudice. It is important for each school to adapt the recommendations based on the needs of their communities, using assessment and evaluation measures throughout their programming to ensure that their work is having the desired results. However, more empirical research is needed to provide a broader body of evidence about how to most effectively prevent and respond to identity-based bullying. I hope to see this body of research expand as more research is conducted within the United Kingdom (where many schools have integrated identity-based bullying into their policies) and as more schools in the United States adopt similar policies.

WHERE DO WE GO FROM HERE?

Movements for educational reform are likely to continue. In the United States, debates about the Common Core curriculum (see Chapter 5) continue, along with calls to reinvigorate the original intention of charter schools (Kahlenberg & Potter, 2014). In 2014, the United Kingdom's first Education Reform Summit was held in London and brought together educators from around the U.K. with the goal of consensus building concerning the future of educational reform (The Education Foundation, n.d.). Students are also advocating for change and for having more agency in decisions impacting their education. In Kentucky, one group of students advocated for their state senate to pass a bill that would allow a high school student to sit on the hiring committees for new superintendents, arguing that they should be allowed to participate more meaningfully in their school's governance (Cheves, 2015). As pressure to reform continues, educators and scholars should consider how they can capitalize on this energy to infuse social justice initiatives and work to dismantle the structures and cultural values that propagate identity-based bullying.

Promoting Social Justice in Schools

Deterring identity-based bullying is just one aspect of schools becoming equitable environments that promote social justice throughout society.

Schools should be careful not to substitute work to prevent identity-based bullying for all other antidiscrimination efforts. They should not assume that by managing identity-based bullying they no longer need to deal with harassment, discrimination, sexual assault, relationship violence, and structural inequalities. Hopefully, an approach to addressing identity-based bullying that centralizes structural changes and social justice will have some ripple effects to promote equity overall, but schools must remain vigilant. The editors at *Rethinking Our Classrooms* provide a hopeful guide for classroom practices to promote social justice (Au, Bigelow, & Karp, 2007). They highlight the need for a curriculum that is multicultural, antiracist, and projustice. Such a curriculum should be academically rigorous, while also being culturally sensitive and positive. They emphasize the use of experiential activities and assert that students should learn to be critical thinkers and activists.

Despite the hard work of educational advocates, many schools continue to be spaces were inequality is reproduced and reinforced. In the United States, the *school-to-prison pipeline* is a term used by educational scholars and activists to describe how some students are pushed out of schooling and into the criminal justice system. This pipeline includes policies that encourage the presence of police officers within schools and zero-tolerance policies (including those used to punish bullying), which lead to increased numbers of out-of-school suspensions and expulsions (Elias, 2013). Ethnic minorities and children with disabilities are disproportionately impacted by these policies and have the highest representation within the pipeline (Elias, 2013). Scholars within the United States have been studying this pipeline for decades, attempting to better understand the factors that create and maintain it (see Osher et al., 2012). Various solutions to this problem have been posed, including the adoption of the Positive Behavioral Interventions and Supports (PBIS) framework to address disciplinary problems (Fenning & Rose, 2007) and the involvement of school-based mental health professionals in examining disciplinary practices within schools (Darensbourg, Perez, & Blake, 2010). One widely advocated for solution involves the adoption of restorative justice approaches (see Chapter 7) as an alternative to zero-tolerance policies (Cregor & Hewitt, 2011; Gonzalez, 2012). Some scholars and educational activists have asserted that the continued racial disparity in the way discipline is enforced indicates a need for a social justice perspective to dismantle the pipeline. In their April 2015 issue, the editors of *Rethinking Schools* called for a *school-to-justice pipeline* to eradicate the policies and social values that have too often resulted in young Black people going to prison or dying at the hands of law enforcement, security guards, or vigilantes (Black Students' Lives Matter, 2015). They call upon educators to use a social justice, anti-racist curriculum to address the enormous detrimental impacts of racism on young people of color.

Dealing with the school-to-prison pipeline is just one example of how schools can expand beyond deterrence of identity-based bullying to create equitable and safe school environments. Promoting social justice within school systems can at times be challenging and draining work, but it can also be inspirational and positive. In his work writing about his experiences as a teacher in urban schools, Yeo (1997) describes the importance of celebrating difference, helping children find joy in their identities, and the ethic of hope—without which it is difficult to envision an approach to education that truly values multiculturalism and strives to eradicate inequity.

Social Justice Beyond the Schoolyard

In this book, I have focused primarily on schools and how they can best prevent and respond to identity-based bullying. In addition to exploring ways that schools can refocus on social justice, it is essential to examine how other social institutions can promote the values of a diverse society. These spaces can be locations where identity-based bullying happens, but they also can become epicenters for change. For example, public libraries can be sites of social change by interrupting societal messages, providing educational opportunities, and supporting social justice initiatives. One small public library in Ferguson, Missouri, was launched onto the national stage during protests following the decision not to indict White police officer Darren Wilson in the fatal shooting of Michael Brown, an unarmed young Black man (Hu, 2014). The library stayed open during a time when many businesses and most schools were closed. They invited people to use the space for discussions, organizational meetings, and just to take a break. They also let people know that the library was a safe place for children to spend their day while their schools were closed. The library offered kids *healing kits*, which included books dealing with traumatic events and a stuffed animal for the children to keep (Hu, 2014). I was inspired as I read about the Ferguson Library and the efforts they were making to be a force for good during a troubling time.

Recently, I found myself in one of the public libraries in Pittsburgh, and I noticed signs posted on the ends of the bookshelves. The statement "We need diverse books because . . ." had been printed on the signs with an open space for individuals to fill in the blank. I was captivated and walked around the entire library reading the entries. Some of the responses that spoke to me included statements like:

- "Open minds = open hearts. Knowledge is power."
- "Everyone deserves to see themselves in characters no matter what."
- "I'm a princess who wants to be saved by a princess."

I asked a librarian about the signs and was informed that the library posted them in honor of LGBTQ pride week. I was incredibly moved by the display and am so appreciative that the library posted them. I wonder how many children and adolescents saw these signs and thought "Maybe I am not alone." Or how many adults read a sign and realized they should have a conversation about diversity with their children or students or community. Obviously no one library campaign or person or book will eradicate identity-based bullying, but every effort is an important step on the path to creating a just society free of discrimination and harassment.

CLOSING THOUGHTS

I know that this book is imperfect. My own life experiences, biases, identities, and education have greatly impacted my choice of subject matter and the lens through which I view it. I anticipate the reader will find new insights, suggestions, or ideas that they can apply to their own work. I also expect that some will find flaws within. I hope readers forgive me these flaws and that they are able to take what they can from this book to inform their own efforts toward bettering the lives of children. I do not contend that I have provided all the answers in this one book, but I hope I have contributed to a conversation in which we are asking the right questions. Because at the end of the day, we will only answer the questions that we ask.

All too often our schools are the spaces where children experience the most fear—it is time for that to change. I believe our educational institutions can become places for healing, places where children feel safe and valued. As educators, counselors, psychologists, and scholars we can expand possibilities, inspire social change, and dismantle systematic oppression. The work does not come easy. But it is up to us to envision the possibility of a just world. Even if it sits upon the horizon—just out of reach—each step we take can move us in the direction of that vision. Sometimes we have to take a deep breath, feel the sunlight on our faces, and keep going forward.

REFERENCES

Au, W., Bigelow, B., & Karp, S. (2007). Introduction: Creating classrooms for equity and social justice. *Rethinking Our Classrooms, 1,* x–xi.

Black students' lives matter: Building the school-to-justice pipeline. (2015, Spring). *Rethinking Schools, 29,* 4–7.

Brinkman, B. G., Jedinak, A., Rosén, L. A., & Zimmerman, T. S. (2011). Teaching children fairness: Decreasing gender prejudice among children. *Analyses of Social Issues and Public Policy, 11,* 61–81. doi: 10.1111/j.1530-2415.2010.01222.x

Brown, C. S., & Bigler, R. S. (2004). Children's perceptions of gender discrimination. *Developmental Psychology, 40,* 714–726.

Brown, L. M., Chesney-Lind, M., & Stein, N. (2007). Patriarchy matters: Toward a gendered theory of teen violence and victimization. *Violence Against Women, 13,* 1249–1273. doi: 10.1177/1077801207310430

Cheves, J. (2015). Proposal to let students help pick superintendents advances to Kentucky Senate. *Lexinton Herald-Leader.* Retrieved from http://www.kentucky.com/2015/03/09/3736103/proposal-to-let-students-help.html

Cregor, M., & Hewitt, D. (2011). Dismantling the school-to-prison pipeline: A survey from the field. *Poverty and Race, 20,* 5–7.

Darensbourg, A., Perez, E., & Blake, J.J. (2010). Overrepresentation of African American males in exclusionary discipline: The role of school-based mental health professionals in dismantling the school to prison pipeline. *Journal of African American Males in Education, 1,* 196–211.

The Education Foundation, (n.d.). Summit 2014. Retrieved from http://www.ednfoundation.org/summit2014/

Elias, M. (2013, Spring). The school-to-prison pipeline: Policies and practices that favor incarceration over education do us all a grave injustice. *Teaching Tolerance,* 39–40.

Farnen, R.F. (2007). Class matters: Inequality, SES, education and childhood in the USA and Canada today. *Policy Futures in Education, 5,* 278–302.

Fenning, P., & Rose, J. (2007). Overrepresentation of African American students in exclusionary discipline: The role of school policy. *Urban Education, 42,* 536–559. doi: 10.1177/0042085907305039

Freire, P. (1970). *Pedagogy of the oppressed.* New York, NY: The Continuum International Publishing Group.

Gonzalez, T. (2012). Keeping kids in schools: Restorative justice, punitive discipline, and the school to prison pipeline. *Journal of Law and Education, 41,* 281–235.

hooks, b. (1994). *Teaching to transgress: Education as the practice of freedom.* New York, NY: Routledge Press.

Hu, E. (2014, November 27). A nationwide outpouring of support for tiny Ferguson library. *National Public Radio.* Retrieved from http://www.npr.org/blogs/thetwo-way/2014/11/27/366811650/a-nationwide-outpouring-of-support-for-tiny-ferguson-library

Jenson, J. M., Dieterich, W. A., Brisson, D., Bender, K. A., & Powell, A. (2010). Preventing childhood bullying: Findings and lessons from the Denver public schools trial. *Research on Social Work Practice, 20,* 509–517.

Kahlenberg, R., & Potter, H. (2014). Restoring Shanker's vision for charter schools. *American Educator, 38*(4), 4–13.

Liu, W. M., Soleck, G., Hopps, J., Dunston, K., & Pickett, T. (2004). A new framework to understand social class in counseling: The social class worldview and modern classism theory. *Journal of Multicultural Counseling and Development, 32,* 95–122. doi: 10.1002/j.2161-1912.2004.tb00364.x

Meyer, E. J. (2009). *Gender, bullying, and harassment: Strategies to end sexism and homophobia in schools.* New York, NY: Teacher's College Press.

Osher, D., Coggshall, J., Colombi, G., Woodruff, D., Francois, S., & Osher, T. (2012). Building school and teacher capacity to eliminate the school-to-prison pipeline. *Teacher Education and Special Education, 35,* 284–295.

Poteat, V.P., & Espelage, D.L. (2005). Exploring the relation between bullying and homophobic verbal content: The homophobic content agent target (HCAT) scale. *Violence and Victims, 20,* 513–528.

Renold, E. (2005). *Girls, boys, and junior sexualities: Exploring children's gender and sexual relations in the primary school.* London: Routledge.

Richardson, R., & Miles, B. (2008). *Racist incidents and bullying in schools.* Staffordshire, UK: Trentham Books Limited.

Russell, S.T., Ryan, C., Toomey, R. B., Diaz, R.M., & Sanchez, J. (2011). Lesbian, gay, bisexual and transgender adolescent school victimization: Implications for young adult health and adjustment. *Journal of School Health, 81,* 223–230.

Tippett, N., Houlston, C., & Smith, P. K. (2010). *Prevention and response to identity-based bullying among local authorities in England, Scotland, and Wales* (Research report 64). London, England: Equality and Human Rights Commission.

Wessler, S. L., & De Andrade, L. L. (2006). Slurs, stereotypes, and student interventions: Examining the dynamics, impact, and prevention of harassment in middle and high school. *Journal of Social Issues, 62,* 511–532. doi: 10.1111/j.1540-4560.2006.00471.x

Yeo, F. L. (1997). *Inner city schools, multiculturalism, and teacher education: A professional journey.* New York, NY: Garland Publishing, Inc.

Appendix
Useful Websites

U.K.

Anti-Bullying Alliance

A coalition of organizations and individuals working together to stop bullying and create safe environments in which children and young people can live, grow, play, and learn.
   www.anti-bullyingalliance.org.uk

Bullying in School

Resources provided by the U.K. government about bullying, laws that apply to bullying, and how to address bullying within schools.
   www.gov.uk/bullying-at-school/the-law

Equality and Human Rights Commission

Organization within Great Britain charged with combating discrimination and working to promote human rights. They conduct research on identity-based bullying within Britain and provide guidance for schools about how to combat it.
   www.equalityhumanrights.com

LGBT Youth Scotland

The largest community-based organization working with LGBT youth in Scotland. They work to empower LGBT youth and provide them with connections and support within the community.
   www.lgbtyouth.org.uk

RespectMe

Scotland's anti-bullying service. The organization provides information about ways to effectively address bullying and harassment against children.
   www.respectme.org.uk

132 *Appendix*

U.S.

Anti-Defamation League

The Anti-Defamation League was founded in the United States to battle anti-Semitism but has expanded its mission to fight for civil rights of various oppressed groups. The organization provides guidance on addressing bias and bullying within schools, anti-bias curriculum that promotes respect and inclusivity, and lesson plans for confronting bigotry.
 www.adl.org/education-outreach

Bullying Research Network

A network that promotes collaboration among scholars conducting research on bullying and victimization of children.
 cehs15.unl.edu/cms/index.php?s=2&p=124 (U.S. with international target)

Coaching Boys into Men (CBIM)

CBIM is a program designed to utilize the relationship between coaches and male athletes to challenge stereotypes about masculinity, especially those that promote aggressive and even violent behavior. The intention is for athletes to learn relational skills to avoid violence and demonstrate respect for girls and women. The program has been used within high schools and middle schools.
 www.coachescorner.org

Fairness for All Individuals through Respect (FAIR)

FAIR is an experientially based curriculum for children that encourages an understanding of social injustice.
 www.fair.chhs.colostate.edu

Gay, Lesbian, and Straight Education Network (GLSEN)

GLSEN works to create safe school environments for all children, especially those who identify as LGBT. They provide resources to support ongoing professional development of staff, as well as curriculum that can be used directly in schools. The resources include guides for various campaigns to do within schools (such as Ally Week), LGBT inclusive curriculum, and support for addressing homophobic bullying in schools.
 glsen.org/educate/resources/curriculum

Hardy Girls, Healthy Women

This nonprofit organization is designed to support the healthy development of girls by focusing on their relational lives and social contexts, providing

education to communities, engaging and empowering girls. Hardy Girls, Healthy Women offers numerous programs, including curriculum that can be adopted in schools to develop coalition groups for middle school girls.
   hghw.org

It Gets Better Project

The It Gets Better Project's mission is to communicate to lesbian, gay, bisexual, and transgender youth around the world that it gets better and to create and inspire the changes needed to make it better for them.
   www.itgetsbetter.org

The Representation Project

This project uses film to educate about gender-role stereotypes (especially within the United States) and the ways in which media represents girls/women and boys/men. In addition to two films (*Miss Representation* and *The Mask You Live In*), the project provides curriculum that can be used at all educational levels to engage students in critical thinking about gender stereotypes and inspire healthier behavior and interpersonal relationships.
   therepresentationproject.org

Rethinking Schools

Rethinking Schools is a nonprofit publisher and advocacy organization dedicated to sustaining and strengthening public education through social justice teaching and educational activism.
   www.rethinkingschools.org

Seeking Educational Equity and Diversity

The National SEED Project on Inclusive Curriculum is the nation's largest peer-led leadership development project. It engages public and private school teachers, college faculty, parents, and community leaders from all subject areas, grade levels, and geographic locations to create gender fair, multiculturally equitable, socioeconomically aware, and globally informed education.
   www.nationalseedproject.org

SPARK Movement

This is a girl-centered activist movement designed to challenge sexualization of girls and women in the media. SPARK offers a curriculum designed for older girls and young women to explore ways to become media activists.
   www.sparksummit.com

Stopbullying.gov

Includes information compiled by the U.S. government about bullying, including how it is defined, policies that apply to bullying, and how to effectively prevent and respond to bullying.

www.stopbullying.gov

Teaching Tolerance

Teaching Tolerance is an organization designed to help educators reduce prejudice and to increase inclusivity and justice within schools. They provide reports with best practices and recommendations for creating inclusive and anti-bias schools. Their anti-bias framework offers learning outcomes in four domains, including identity, diversity, justice, and action. They have numerous resources for activities, lesson plans, films, and discussions that can be used in the classroom.

www.tolerance.org

The UnSlut project

The UnSlut Project promotes gender equality, sex positivity, and comprehensive, age-appropriate sex education for all ages.

www.unslutproject.com

Index

Aboud, F. E. 44, 104
Abrams, D. 44, 49
academic environment, assessing 114, 116
activism, student engagement in 50
adequate yearly progress (AYP) 76
adults: engaging 93–8, 99; lack of support from 111–12; *see also* educators; parents
affective environment, assessing 114, 115–16
African Americans: harassment and bullying of 11; high school graduation rates for 28; impact of discrimination on 30–1; internalizing negative Black stereotypes 46–7; upward mobility opportunities for 24–5; *see also* Blacks
aggression: bullying and 4; relational 8
Alabi, B. O. 6, 46, 92
Aleman, E. 33–4
Alexander, R. J. 34–5
American Association of University Women study 7
American Psychological Association reports, on social aspects of identity 25–6
Americans with Disabilities Act, Title II of 79
A Nation at Risk 73
Anderson, S. 93, 98, 105, 111, 113
And Tango Makes Three 60
Anti-Bullying Alliance 131
anti-bullying interventions/policies 1, 81, 98–9; for adult bystanders 93–8, 99; in charter schools 75; engaging students in 91–3; expertise in 87–8; focusing on social identities 2–3; focusing on victim vulnerability 43; funding for 86–7; impact of 88–90; literature on 102–3; parents' reactions to 97–8; putting recommendations into action 107–18; resources for 84–8, 105; ripple effects of 84; school culture and 34–5, 40, 117; strategic planning for 106–7; student resistance to 91–2; team building for 105–6; utilizing research evidence in 102–5
Anti-Defamation League 113, 132
antidiscrimination efforts 125–6
Arab-descent children: bullying against 63; bullying of related to Islamophobia 94–5
Ashburn-Nardo, L. 93
Asian Americans, model minority stereotype of 11
Association for Women in Psychology, on social justice 26
autism spectrum 13
Awad, G. H. 33

Bailey, T. K. M. 46, 47
behaviors, avoiding 46–7, 49
Bell, L. A. 22, 104
Bender, K. A. 2, 89, 123
Bergman, B. J. 117
Berliner, D. 85
Bickmore, K. 88
Bigelow, B. 76, 126
Bigler, R. S. 6, 116, 123
Blacks: anti-bullying interventions for 108; in school-to-prison pipeline 126; zero tolerance policies applied to 90; *see also* African Americans
Black Students' Lives Matter 126

Index

Borgida, E. 44, 45
Borooah, V. 65
Bosson, J. K. 48
Bream, V. 2, 97–8
Bring it On 59
Brinkman, B. G. 2–3, 11, 46, 75, 104, 111, 123
Brisson, D. 2, 89, 123
Brofenbrenner, U., ecological system theory of 39
Brown, C. S. 3, 5, 6, 8, 11, 15, 46, 48, 92, 123
Brown, H. 57
Brown, L. M. 43, 58, 90, 117, 123
Brown, Michael, fatal shooting of 127
Brown, R. 103
Brown v. Board of Education 28
Buchanan, A. 2, 97–8
Buhin, L. 22
bullies: labeling 43, 91; punishing 89, 90
bullying 3–15; adults' experience of 15–6; circumstances of 43; discrimination and 89–90; functions of 14–15; versus harassment 4–6; homophobic 1, 5–6; identity-based versus other forms of 109–10; incidence of 2; negative consequences of 2; online 2; prevention of 1–2; reason for concern about 1–3; religion-based 65; school climate reinforcing 114–15; settings for 16; violent response to 1; *see also* class-based bullying; gender-based bullying; identity-based bullying; prejudice-based bullying; racial-based bullying
bullying behavior: awareness of 93–4; cost-benefits of intervening in 96–7; determining harmfulness of 94–5; taking responsibility for intervening in 95–7
Bullying Prevention Summit of 2010, 79
Bullying Research Network 132
Bullying in School 131
Burgess, D. 44, 45
Burgess, S. 74
Burke, C. 50
Burnaford, R. M. 48
Burrow, A. L. 64
Butler Act 72

bystander interventions 93–8, 99; barriers to 111–12
bystanders 15; supporting bullying 111

Charlie Hebdo, terrorist attack on 117
chav 58–9, 108–9
Chesir-Teran, D. 29, 81
Chesney-Lind, M. 3, 43, 90, 123
Cheves, J. 125
children: as active agents 41, 42–4, 50; creating social change 49–50; excluding from identity discussions 49–50; marketing to 58
Children's Manifesto 50
Chung, Y. B. 46
Civil Rights, Office for: call for school anti-bullying programs by 79–80; *Dear Colleague* letter issued by 79
Civil Rights Act of 1964, 79
civil rights movement 28
Civil Rights Project 87
Clark, K. B. 28
Clark, M. K. 28
class: markers of 56; media portrayals of 57–9
class-based bullying 12–13, 109–10; ads promoting 58; interventions for 108–9
class-based conflict 55–6
class-based prejudice 55–9
classism: downward 12; internalized 56; interpersonal 47; lateral 12; upward 12
Claudius, M. 31
Clinton, Bill 57
clubs, empowerment 115–16
Coaching Boys into Men 112, 132
co-intentional education model 50
Cole, E. R. 24
Coleman Report 73
Collins, A. 41
colorblindness 33–4
Columbine High School shooting 1; bullying experience in 2
Common Core 77
Confronting Prejudiced Responses Model (CPR), 93–8
Connell, R. W. 22
constructivism *see* social constructivism; social constructivist theory
Copeland-Linder, N. 11, 30–1
Crenshaw, K. W. 90

Crick, N. R. 8
critical thinking skills 34
Crothers, L. M. 8
Crowe, K. 58
cultural attitudes, programs to shift 117–8; stereotypical 5
cultural influences 55, 65–6, 116–8, 124; ethnicity and 62–5; gender and 59–62; poverty and 55–9; religious 65
curriculum: hidden 33, 81; high-stakes testing impact on 85; multicultural and projustice 126; social justice and antiracist 113; SPARK 117
cyberbullying 16, 95

Dacus, B. 98
Davuluri, Nina (Miss America) 63
De Andrade, L. L. 2, 123
Defense of Marriage Act (DOMA), ruling against 59
depression 32
Derman-Sparks, L. 44
descriptive stereotypes 44–5
desegregation, school 28
Dessel, A. 116
Dewitt, P. 5, 105, 113
Diaz, E. M. 9, 32
Diaz, R. M. 115, 123
Dieterich, W. A. 2, 89, 123
DiGiovanni, C. D. 115
disabilities 13–14; bullying and 6; physical 13–14
discipline, racial differences in 29
discrimination: bullying and 89–90; class-based 12; ethnic 11; versus identity-based bullying 4, 109–10; impact of 30–1; student awareness of 92
discriminatory beliefs: factors contributing to 44; leading to identity-based bullying 44–5
disenfranchised, inclusion of 110–11
diversity training 87–8
Donne, John, *Meditation XVII* of 66
Dovidio, J. F. 44
Du Bois, C. 24
Duck Dynasty 62
Duke, T. S. 104, 116
Duncan, N. 6, 7, 9, 30, 47, 97
Dunston, K. 12, 48, 56, 123

Eagly, A. H. 44
ecological systems theory 39
economic inequality, schools reinforcing 28
Eder, D. 7, 27, 48
Education, Department of 72, 79–80
Education, Ministry of 72–3
Education Act of 1930 (Northern Ireland) 65
educational inequality 28
educational/school reform: movements for 125; new vision for 78
Education Reform Act of 1988 (U.K.) 72–3
Education Reform Summit (U.K.) 125
education systems 70–1, 81–2; climate of 80–1; reform movements in 73–8; U.K. laws impacting bullying in 80; in United Kingdom 72–3; in United States 71–2; U.S. laws impacting bullying in 78–80
educators: challenging stereotypes 113; legal responsibilities of 95–6; professional development for 113; social identities of 97; training for 116; using restorative justice 113–14
empathy 103
empowerment groups 115–16
English language learners 75, 88
environmental conditions 43
Epstein, T. 24
equality, complex 22–3
Equality Act 2010, 80
Equality and Human Rights Commission (EHRC), 80, 88, 96, 131; report of 3–4
Erford, B. T. 26
Erikson, E. H. 16
Eslea, M. 11, 12
Espelage, D. L. 2, 5, 10, 14, 39, 40, 89, 103, 104, 105, 111, 123
ethnicity 11; developing identity with 46; gender and 6; racism and diversity of 103–4; religion and 11–12; training for discussions of 116
ethnic solidarity 33
Evans, C. C. 7, 8, 27, 48
exclusion, negative impact of 94
exosystem 39
experiences, limiting exposure to 46–7

138 *Index*

FAIR Education Act 79
Fairness for All Individuals through Respect (FAIR), 2–3, 104, 112, 132
Farnen, R. F. 76, 124
femininity stereotypes 9
feminist perspective, on social justice 23–4, 25
Fenning, P. 126
Ferguson Library, healing kits offered by 127–8
financial challenges 86–7
Fishbein, H. D. 45
Foster Act 72
Foud, N. 26
Frankenberg, E. 33, 87
Fredrickson, B. L. 47
Freire, P. 26, 27, 50, 123
Fried, S. 5, 14, 43, 110–1
Friedman, M. S. 1

gay, as slur 10–1
Gay, Lesbian, and Straight Education Network (GLSEN) 132
gay individuals: accepting negative gay stereotypes 46–7; boys' prejudicial attitudes toward 45; bullying of 10; media depictions of 61–2
Gay-Straight Alliances 10, 50, 81, 115
gender: deemphasizing differences of 115; nonheteronormative expression of 115; performance of 48–9; race and 6
gender-based bullying 6–10, 109–10; of boys 8–9; bystander interventions for 111–2; of girls 7–8; impact of 32; masculinity and 6; negative impact of 94; self-objectification of victims of 47
gender identity 6–10; nonconforming 9–10
gender-inclusiveness 108
gender nonconforming individuals: male versus female 9–10; portrayed in media 61–2
gender prejudice, reduction of 104
gender roles: challenging 48; expectations impacting 48; nonconformity to 91
gender stereotypes 27–8, 97; challenging 113; conformity to 47–8; media reinforcing 117; programs addressing 112

Gerstein, L. 26
Gibbons, F. X. 30
Girls Coalition Groups 117
Goodenow, C. 81–2
Graham, S. 103–4
Green, J. E. 65, 71, 72, 73
Gregen, Kenneth 41
guycode 48

harassment: versus bullying 4–6; definition of 5; discriminatory 5; escalation of 29; versus identity-based bullying 109–10; of LGB students 10–11; negative impact of 94–5; sexual 6–7; *see also* sexual harassment
Harber, C. 8, 26–7, 81
Hardy Girls, Healthy Women 117, 132–3
Hayes, D. M. 97, 116
Heinemann, K. S. 103
Heinze, J. E. 9–10
Hemming, J. 91
Here Comes Honey Boo Boo 58
heterosexuality: failing at 9; nonconformity to 60–1, 86; as norm 27–8, 31, 32–3, 115; privilege of 23–4
Hewitt, D. 126
hierarchy, culture of 29
Higgins, H. J. 85
high-stakes testing: impact on curriculum of 85; in the United Kingdom 77; in the United States 75–7
Hill, N. E. 24
Hinduja, S. 16, 81, 95, 114–15
Holcomb, S. 12, 63, 95
homophobia 5; in boys 45; bullying and 1, 5–6; masculinity and 8; prejudice reduction approaches to 104
homophobic teasing 9
Hong, L. 105
hooks, bell 25, 123
Hopps, J. 12, 48, 56, 123
Horn, S. S. 9–10
Horne, A. M. 4, 5, 14, 26, 43, 110, 112, 116
Houlston, C. 3–4, 80, 88, 124
Hughes, D. 29, 81
Hughes, J. 65
Huynh, V. W. 6, 46, 92
Hymel, S. 2, 89, 104
hyper-masculinity 31–2

identity: changing 24–5; formation of 46, 47–8; hiding aspects of 48; intersecting with bullying 6, 89
identity-based bullying: ability/disability-based 13–14; adult bystanders to 93–8; appropriately labeling 109–10; challenges to addressing 17; contextual variables impacting 124; CPR Model approach to 93–7; creating and reinforcing inequality 29–30; cultural influences on 17, 55–66; definition of 3–4; ethnicity, nationality, and religion based 11–2; gender and 6–10; impact of 30–2; internalized stereotypes in 46–9; perpetrators of 14–15; political and structural factors in 17; prejudice and discriminatory beliefs in 44–5; prevention of 17; recognizing as potentially harmful 94–5; school climate and culture in 80–1; sexual orientation-based 1, 10–11; social class-based 12–13; social constructivist approach to 41–2; social-ecological model of 39–40; societal and cultural influences on 116–18; theoretical basis of 16–17; U.K. laws impacting 80; in U.K. versus U.S. 16; U.S. laws impacting 78–80
Illich, I. 27
immigrants, post-9/11 treatment of 63–4
immigration 62–4
impairments, mimicking of 14
inclusive language 115
inequality: identity-based bullying in 29–30; patriarchy and 23–4; in schools 26–9
in-person interactions 16
instigators 15
intergroup contact 45, 103–4
interventions *see* anti-bullying interventions/policies
invisible norm 28, 33
Irish immigrants, discrimination against 25
Isacco, A. 22
Isava, D.M. 102
Islamophobia 94–5
Israel, T. 26
It Gets Better Project 133

Jackson, P. W. 27, 33
Jedinak, A. 2–3, 104, 123
Jenson, J. M. 2, 89, 123
justice, definition of 22

Kahlenberg, R. 125
Karp, S. 76, 126
Katz, J, 2
Kellner, D. 76
Killen, M. 44, 49
Kimmel, M. S. 2, 8, 29, 45, 47, 48, 112
Kirshner, B. 117
Klein, J. 2, 7, 8, 12, 31, 34, 45, 56, 90, 94, 114

labeling 91–2
Lamb, S. 7, 58
Latinos: high school graduation rates for 28; upward mobility opportunities for 24
Leachman, M. 86
learning opportunities 113
Lee, H. Y. 103
legal issues: about sexual harassment 7, 78; anti-bullying 80–2; anti-discrimination 79–80; impacting identity-based bullying 85, 87, 95–8, 124; in United Kingdom 80; in United States 78–80
lesbians: bullying of 10, 60; girls' prejudicial attitudes toward 45; supporting social justice 50; victimization of 2
Lewis, R. L. 11, 30–1
Lexton, L. 58
LGB individuals: bullying impact on 31–2; bullying of 10–11; stereotypes of 96; vicarious victimization of 29–30
LGBT friendly programs 81
LGBT individuals: accepting negative gay stereotypes 46–7; bullying and harassment of 9–10; laws protecting 79; stereotypical attitudes toward 45; value neutral policy toward 32–3
LGBTQ educators 97
LGBTQ individuals: affective environment for 115–16; legal rights for 59–62; media representations of 61–2
LGBT Youth Scotland 131

Liben, L. S. 6
Limber, S. P. 89
literature: LGBTQ individuals in 60; multicultural 33
Liu, W. M. 12, 48, 56, 123
Livingston, J. A. 107
local education agencies (LEAs), 73
Lynn Report 65

Ma, X. 14, 15, 40
McCarthy, K. W. 104, 116
MacIntosh, R. 47
McNamara, B. E. 6, 13, 14, 104, 105, 107, 112
macrosystem 39
Mahler, M. 2, 112
Manning, L. 11, 75, 111
Mansaray, A. 24
marginalized groups, upward mobility opportunities for 24–5
marketers, targeting children 58
Marley, D. 77
Marriage (Same Sex Couples) Act (UK), 61
Marshall, Thurgood 28
Martin, C. L. 116
Martin, P. P. 11, 26, 30–1
masculinity: alternative definitions of 34; bullying to affirm 14; challenging stereotypes about 113; dominance and 7–8; gender-based bullying and 6; hegemonic 8, 27–8, 45, 112; nonconformity to 31–2; stereotypical 8–9, 47–8; violence and 2
Masten, C. L. 6, 46, 92
Maylor, U. 87
meaning-making process 41–2
media: influencing identity-based bullying 117; LGBTQ individuals represented in 61–2; social class in 57–9; transgender individuals in 62
Medicaid 57
mesosystem 39
Meyer, E. J. 3, 5–6, 105, 106–7, 109, 123
Michalscheck, A. 61
microaggressions 33
Middle Eastern immigrants, post-9/11 treatment of 11–12, 63–4; *see also* Muslims

Miles, B. 6, 50, 88, 105, 113–14, 116, 123
minimum wage, raising 56–7
Misfits 58–9
Mishna, F. 16, 31, 46, 94
model minority stereotype 11
Modern Family 61–2
Moradi, B. 47
Morris, K. A. 93
Mukhtar, K. 11, 12
Multicultural Education, Five Key Dimensions of 34–5
multiculturalism: in education 34–5; promoting 81, 127
multicultural literature 33
Muslims: anti-bullying interventions for 108; bullying of 63; harassment of 117–18; Islamophobia and bullying of 94–5; post-9/11 treatment of 11–12, 63–4

Nansel, T. 2, 43
Napolitano, S. A. 105
National Association of School Psychologists, on LGBT youth 26
nationality 11
negatively stereotyped groups: developing identity with 46; internalizing negative stereotypes 46–8
Newman, D. 16, 23
No Child Left Behind 70; mandating school safety 81–2; policies of 71
No Child Left Behind Act 76; impact on curriculum of 85
Northern Ireland: national educational curriculum in 73; religion and bullying in 65
Norwich, B. 13, 14

Obama, Barack: election of 34; as first African American president 64; hosting anti-bullying conference 1–2; minimum wage policy of 56; on same-sex marriage 60
Obama administration: Bullying Prevention Summit of 79; Race to the Top program of 77
Ocen, P. 90
O'Connell, P. 15
O'Connor, A. 1
Office for Standards in Education (OFSTED), 72 80

Office of Civil Rights (OCR), enforcing discrimination laws 95–6
Olen, H. 58
Olweus, D. 4, 39, 89
Olweus Bullying Prevention Program 88–9
Omari, S. R. 24
Ong, A. D. 64
oppression: internalized 47; racial 44, 74; systemic/institutional 26, 30, 94–5, 115–16, 128
Orange Is the New Black 62
Orpinas, P. 4, 5, 14, 26, 43, 110, 112, 116

Page, S. E. 105
Pahl, K. 30, 46
parents: in anti-bullying interventions 43, 51, 97–8; influence of 44; opposing ads targeting children 58; opposing social identity discussions 98; same-sex 60
Parker, L. 33–4
Pascoe, C. J. 9, 10–11, 27, 31, 43, 49–50, 109, 115
Patchin, J. W. 16, 81, 95, 114–15
patriarchy, inequality and 23–4
Pedagogy of the Oppressed 123
peer groups, bullying behavior in 43
peers, bullying by 14
Pendragon, D. K. 10, 50
perpetrators 15
Personal Responsibility and Work Opportunity Reconciliation Act 57
perspective taking 103
Pettigrew, T. F. 28, 45, 103
Phillips, C. B. 44
physical violence 10, 13, 29, 63
Pickett, T. E. 12, 48, 56, 123
policies *see* anti-bullying interventions/policies
Pollack, W. S. 8, 32, 45, 47, 112
poor: in media 57–9; prejudice against 55–9; social policies impacting 56–7; stigmatizing of 57
Positive Behavioral Interventions and Supports (PBIS) framework 126
post-bystanderism stage 113
post-racial America 64
Poteat, V. P. 10, 115, 123
Potter, H. 125
Poverty Tour 59

Powell, A. 2, 89, 123
Powell, D. 85
power-control scenarios 89
power differentials 4–5, 43–4
power relations 4–5
pre-bystanderism stage 111–12
precarious manhood 47–8
prejudice: leading to identity-based bullying 44–5; against poor 55–9; *see also* classism; discrimination; racism
prejudice-based bullying 3–4, 5; *see also* identity-based bullying
prejudice reduction approaches 103–4
prescriptive stereotypes 44–5
prevention strategies 112–14
privilege 23–4, 33; reluctance to give up 92–3
privilege walk 92
proactive strategies 112–14
Prophet Mohamed cartoons 117
prosocial norms, internalization of 39–40
"provocative" victims 13
public schools, funding for 71–2
punishment, versus restorative justice 113–14

Quart, A. 58

Rabenstein, K. 46
race: gender and 6; training for discussions of 116
Race to the Top program 71, 77
racial-based bullying 11; religion and 11–12; in U.K. after 9/11 attacks 63–4; in U.S. after 9/11 attacks 63; in U.S. versus U.K. 63
racial discrimination, impact of 30–1
racism 5; bullying and 6; curricula opposing 126; ethnic diversity reducing 103–4
Raskin, J. D. 41, 46
Ravitch, D. 71, 73, 74, 75, 76
reading comprehension practice, topics in 86
Rehabilitation Act of 1973, Section 504 of 79
relational aggression 8
religion 11–12; bullying and 65
Renold, E. 3, 5, 109, 110, 123
repetitive bullying behaviors 89–90
Representation Project, The 117, 133

research evidence, utilizing 102–5
resources 84–5; for bullying prevention 105; changing distribution of 24–5; expertise 87–8; financial 86–7; time 85–6; unequal distribution of 23
RespectMe 131
restorative justice 113–14
Rethinking Our Classrooms 126
Rethinking Schools 126
Rethinking Schools website 133
Richardson, C. 6, 10
Richardson, R. 50, 88, 105, 113–14, 116, 123
Rigby, K. 4
Ringrose, J. 3, 5, 109, 110
Rodmeyer, Jamey, suicide of 1
Roediger, D. R. 25
roles, labeling of 42–3
Rorrer, A. 33–4
Rosén, L. A. 2–3, 46, 104, 123
rough play 5
Roysircar, G. 26
Russell, S. T. 9, 32, 115, 123
Rutland, A. 103
Ryan, C. 32, 115, 123

Sacirbey, O. 63, 95
Safe Schools Improvement Act 79
Salazar, T. 33–4
Salmivalli, C. 102
Sameroff, A. 31
same-sex marriage: legalization of 59–60; media depictions of 61–2; policies on 60–1
Sanchez, J. 32, 123
Sauntson, H. 33
Savage, Dan 105
school: violence in 1
school boards 72
school of choice policies 74–5
schools: assessing and changing environment of 114–16; "banking" model of 27; charter and private 28–9, 75; class divisions in 59; desegregation of 28; elementary/preschool 7, 71–2; lottery system for 75; reproducing economic inequalities 29; reproducing gender stereotypes 27–8; reproducing social order 26–8; rethinking role of 34–5; segregation in 74–5; social justice role of 22; value neutral policies of 32–4; violence in 1, 2, 31–2
school shootings, identity-based bullying and 31–2
school-to-justice pipeline 126
school-to-prison pipeline 126–7
Schorr, D. 64
Scotland, national educational curriculum in 73
Seeking Educational Equity and Diversity (SEED) project 123, 133
segregation 28, 74–5
self-objectification 47
Sellers, R. M. 11, 30–1
September 11 attack 63
sexism 5, 7; bullying and 5–6
Sexton, T. L. 41
sexual diversity, value neutral policy toward 32–3
sexual double standard 7
sexual harassment 6–7; versus identity-based bullying 109–10; impact of 31; incidence of 7; negative impact of 94; in peer groups 43; U.S. laws against 79
Sexual Harassment and Bullying (Strauss) 95
sexuality, nonheteronormative expression of 115
sexual orientation 10–1; bullying based on 9; treatment of 96
Shepherd, S. 1–2
slut bashing 7
slut shaming 7, 108–9, 110
Smiley, Tavis 59
Smith, E. 32, 50, 70, 71
Smith, P. K. 3–4, 11, 25, 80, 88, 102, 124
social change, children creating 49–50
social class 12–13; *see also* class; class-based bullying; classism
social constructionism 41; *see also* social constructivism
social constructivism 41–2; theory of 50–1
social-ecological model 39–40
social environment, assessing 114–15
social identities 2–3
social inequalities, schools reinforcing 28
social influences 116–18, 124; in identity-based bullying 43

social justice: bystander interventions in 93–8, 99; definition of 22–6; feminist perspective on 23–4, 25; identity-based bullying and 22, 30–2; as means for change 25–6; promoting beyond schoolyard 127–8; promoting in schools 32–5, 125–7; psychological perspective on 25–6
social justice curriculum 113
social justice program 3, 123–4; in charter schools 75; engaging students in 91–3; student resistance to 91–2
social media, harassment on 95
social norms: conformity to 10; internalizing 39–40; in oppression of marginalized groups 35; nonconformity to 91
social order, schools reinforcing 26–9
Society for the Psychological Study of Social Issues, advocating for social justice 26
Society of Counseling Psychology 26
Soleck, G. 12, 48, 56, 123
Soslan, B. 5, 14, 43, 110–11
Southern Poverty Law Center, diversity training program of 87
SPARK Movement 86, 117, 133
Spurgeon, A. 15
stakeholders, engaging multiple 110–12
status markers 12
Stein, N. 3, 43, 90, 123
Stephen, P. 7, 8, 27, 48
stereotypes: about poor 56; internalization of 45, 46–9, 56; schools reinforcing 27–8; social justice curriculum challenging 113
Stern, B. B. 11
Stopbullying.gov 134
Stormshak, E. A. 46
Stover, D. 80–1
strategic planning 106–7
Strauss, S. 5, 6–7, 9, 10, 27, 29, 31, 93–95, 97, 106
Stringer, M. 12
Strong, K. H. 114
Stuber, J. 57
Student Non-Discrimination Act 79
Sue, D. W. 33
suicides 1, 32
Sullivan, K. 105, 111

Swearer, S. M. 2, 5, 14, 32, 39, 40, 89, 104, 105
Szalacha, L. 81–2

Tanenbaum, L. 7
targets 5, 7–11, 15
Taylor, M. 11, 28
teachable moments 113
teachers *see* educators
Teaching Tolerance 113, 134
Teaching to Transgress 123
team building 105–6
teasing 6; homophobic 9, 10; class-based 13, 56; disabilities-based 13–4; negative impact of 94; playful 5
technology gap 24
television: LGBTQ individuals represented on 61–2; poor depicted on 58–9; transgender individuals on 62
Temporary Assistance to Needy Families (TANF), 57
Tenenbaum, H. R. 64
Terrell, H. 46
terrorist, label of 63–4, 117–18
time limitations 85–6
Tippett, N. 3–4, 80, 88, 124
Title IX, 78–9
Tolman, D. 7, 117
tomboys 10
Toomey, R. B. 9, 32, 115, 123
training, for anti-bullying interventions 87–8
Transforming School Counseling Initiative 26
transgender identity 9–10, 62
Transparent 62
Tropp, L. R. 45, 103
troublemakers 91
Tummala-Narra 31
Turner, R. K. 6, 32

UnSlut Project 134
upward mobility 24–5
U.S. Census Bureau, poverty statistics of 56

Vaillancourt, T. 2, 89, 104
value neutral policies 32–4
vicarious victimization 29–30
victims 15; blaming 43–4, 47; victimizing 30

violence, masculinity and 2
Vygotsky, Lev 41

Walters, A. S. 97, 116
War on Terror 63–4
Way, N. 30, 46
Weber, K. 28, 75, 76
websites: U.K. 131; U.S. 132–4
Weishuhn, Kenneth, suicide 1
welfare reform 57
Wessler, S. L. 2, 123
West, Cornell 48–9, 59
Westheimer, K. 81–2
White/European Americans: awareness of discrimination in 92; high school graduation rates for 28; stereotypical attitudes of 45

White House anti-bullying conference 1–2
whiteness: creation of 25; masked 33
white privilege 33
"white trash" 108–9
whole-school approach 104
Wiseman, R. 8
Women on the Map project 86
working class 6, 12, 24, 58–9, 108, 116

Yeager, D. S. 103

zero tolerance policies 90; alternatives to 126
Zimmerman, D. H. 48–9
Zimmerman, T. S. 2–3, 46, 104, 123